Strip&Knit
with STYLE

Mark Hordyszynski

Create Fabric-Yarn

Use Cotton, Wool, Fleece & More

Knit 16 Projects for You & Your Home

C&T PUBLISHING

Publisher: **Amy Marson**

Creative Director: **Gailen Runge**

Acquisitions Editor: **Jan Grigsby**

Editor: **Lynn Koolish**

Technical Editors: **Nanette S. Zeller** and **Robyn Gronning**

Copyeditor/Proofreader: **Wordfirm Inc.**

Cover Designer: **Kristy K. Zacharias**

Book Designer: **Rose Sheifer-Wright**

Production Coordinator: **Tim Manibusan**

Illustrator: **John Heisch**

Photography by **Luke Mulks** and **Diane Pedersen** of C&T Publishing unless otherwise noted

Published by C&T Publishing, Inc., P.O. Box 1456, Lafayette, CA 94549

Library of Congress Cataloging-in-Publication Data

Hordyszynski, Mark
 Strip & knit with style : create fabric-yarn, use cotton, wool, fleece & more : knit 16 projects for you & your home / Mark Hordyszynski.
    p. cm.
 Summary: "Knit 16 fun, fashion-forward wearables and home accessories with strips of cotton, wool, fleece, and other fabrics"—Provided by publisher.
 ISBN 978-1-57120-454-7 (paper trade : alk. paper)
 1. Knitting—Patterns. I. Title. II. Title: Strip and knit with style.

TT825.H665 2009
746.43'2041—dc22   2008014081

Printed in China

10 9 8 7 6 5 4 3 2 1

Contents

Dedication

To all the quilters, fabric crafters, and readers who use a needle and thread—take your sewing machine and hand skills on a new adventure, and purchase your first pair of knitting needles.

To all the knitters, fiber artists, and readers who use needles and yarn—discover the ease of using a rotary cutter, mat, and ruler to create one-of-a-kind handmade fabric-yarns to ply using your knitting know-how.

And especially to all the readers without any knowledge of sewing or knitting—embark on a new crafting journey, and discover a hobby that transcends the borders of knitting and fabric, sewing and yarn.

Acknowledgments

I would like to express my sincerest thanks to the following people. Thank you for making this book possible.

To my mother, who knit me beautiful sweaters with love in every stitch. She tried to teach me to knit, but unfortunately I wasn't an apt pupil.

To Anne Post, who made sure I got the knack of knitting—and, once I did, I was off.

To my business partner, Samantha, who truly is like the Force, for she manages to keep me from spinning out of orbit and crashing into the sun, and binds it all together.

To Marinda Stewart, who is the best friend and mentor any creative person could have. She is a profound, freely giving source of knowledge and a wonderfully intuitive sounding board.

To Olivia Booth, for her perseverance in making the Olivia Top despite her allergic reaction to the fabric-yarn I gave her to knit with.

To Pam and the people at Alto's, for providing a QuiltCut2 system for me to use.

To Harry of Dill Buttons, for getting me the buttons I needed, even though what I wanted was out of the norm.

To Mary and Scott Flanigan, who were an inspiration with their overdyed and felted woolens.

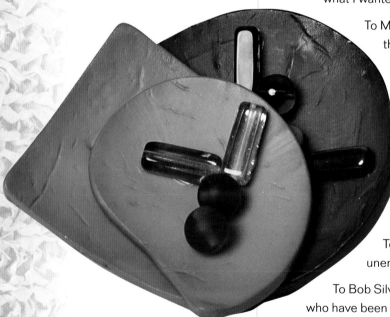

To Ted Finkelstein of Gütermann, for the incredible supply of beads.

To Bruce of Lantern Moon, for the gorgeous exotic wood knitting needles, balls of silk Gelato, and rice baskets.

To Theresa of Princess Mirah Fabrics, for the samples of precut fabric strips for knitting and crocheting.

To Patti Lee at Sulky, who fulfilled my requests for an unending supply of incredibly inspiring threads.

To Bob Silverman and Jim Helms of Woodstock Quilt Supply, who have been supporting me for years by stocking the complete collection of the Fairy Frost fabric.

To the staff at Rosen & Chadick in New York City, for being such helpful and genuinely nice people.

To the C&T Publishing team assigned to this project—if it weren't for them, you wouldn't be holding this book in your hands right now.

Preface

My first experience with knitting with fabric was about a dozen years ago. I was the assistant designer for a men's knitwear business in New York City, in charge of development for the company's largest private-label account. Deconstructionism was in, and ribbed knits in every variation were all the rage. I designed a sweater from strips of muslin. It was a large-ribbed mock turtleneck, slouchy, with reverse seams, and it was very well accepted by my customers and my peers. Unfortunately, its mass-market appeal wasn't so outstanding.

Ten years later, we were celebrating the fifth anniversary of Fairy Frost, one of my cotton fabric collections. I had a booth at Quilt Market in Houston, for which I was designing and making products from the fabric collection. I am an experienced sewer, and I was knocking out projects left and right that were sure to stir excitement and visually impress. But I wanted something unique, different, and interesting, yet not completely out of the norm. Knitting was second nature to me, and I was seeing its resurgence, so I decided to knit a few samples for the booth. Simple, straight-cut strips of fabric were tied together to make a fabric-yarn that was knit into a scarf and two pillows.

And that was the beginning of a craze. Out of almost 50 items in the booth, it was these knitted samples that evoked the most spectacle, buzz, and excitement.

I embarked on a most incredible year of exploration and learning. The journey has been extensive, harrowing, and liberating, allowing me to experiment with color, texture, and pattern—all things that really get my creative juices flowing.

Contained within the pages of this book is everything you need to take your own creative journey. I hope you have as much fun making the projects as I have had designing them. I encourage self-expression and give room in the instructions for personal choices. Enjoy making your one-of-a-kind creations by knitting with fabric-yarn!

Fabric Preparation

Choosing fabrics for your fabric-yarn knitting projects is one of the most exciting steps in the creative process. Even after you fall in love with a particular fabric, the fascination changes as you cut it into strips and reassemble it into one continuous length of fabric-yarn. It changes yet again when it is knit into a project. The technique, in many respects, is similar to quilting, where pieces of fabric are cut up and reassembled into a single stitched piece.

Woven Fabric versus Knit Fabric

Two types of fabrics are used for the projects in this book: woven and knit. Each different fabric has a characteristic look when knit. The type of fabric also affects the gauge and the yardage requirements.

Woven and knit fabrics

Strips from knit fabrics stretch.

Woven fabrics have little or no stretch and can be cut on the lengthwise or crosswise grain. Fabric-yarn made from woven fabric is quite stable. Items knit from this material will keep their shape.

Knit fabrics are naturally stretchy and must be cut crosswise; if they are cut lengthwise (or on the bias) they will pull apart and disintegrate. Depending on the fabric, cut strips can stretch to two or three times their original length, or they can shrink to half their cut length. Using knit fabrics to make fabric-yarn yields narrow fabric-yarn, which can be plied for tweed effects while knitting.

Fabric-yarns made from knit fabrics are stretchy and spongy and will shrink when knit. Knit loosely when using fabric-yarns made from knit fabrics, and, for the same reasons, use great care when mixing woven and knit fabric-yarns.

The Perry—Zebra Stripe Intarsia Pillow (page 54) is made of woven and knit fabric-yarn.

Fabrics for Knitting

The instructions for each project indicate whether the fabric should be cut lengthwise or crosswise. For best results, be sure to follow these recommendations.

Cotton

Cotton is a wonderful, natural fabric. It is easy to work with and readily available. Fabric and quilting stores carry cottons in a variety of colors and patterns. Cotton can have a soft or sturdy hand and is suitable for many projects in this book.

Cotton washes easily and can be cared for without much trouble. To prepare cotton fabrics for making fabric-yarn, rinse the fabric to remove any sizing or residue, and iron the damp fabric on the wrong side to steam out the wrinkles.

Cotton fabrics

Rayon

Rayon is also considered a natural fiber because it is made from cellulose. It has a wonderful drape and can have a soft or crisp hand. Most rayon fabric produced today is machine washable, which makes this another easy-to-care-for fabric.

Rayons should be reserved for projects requiring a great deal of fluid drape, such as garments, and should be used in limited quantities in other projects. To prepare rayon fabrics for making fabric-yarn, gently steam the fabrics to remove any wrinkles.

Rayon fabrics

Linen and Vegetable Fibers

Linen, ramie, hemp, flax, and sisal are natural fibers that can be woven into fabric ranging from handkerchief weight to heavily textured burlap. To prepare these fabrics for making fabric-yarn, spray the fabric using a spray bottle filled with water, and iron or hang to dry.

Unless a linen or linen-like fabric is specified in a specific project, consider the hand of the fabric. Some of these fabrics can get a bit coarse and raspy feeling—great for decorative pieces, but not so appropriate for something you will wear or handle.

Linen and natural vegetable fiber fabrics

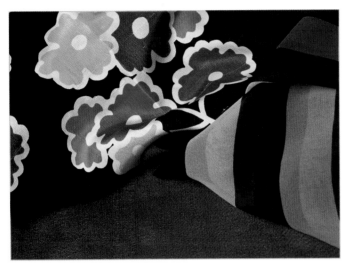
Silk fabrics

Woolen fabrics

Polyester and nylon fabrics

Silk

Made from cocoon filaments of the silk worm, silk is available in weights ranging from fine, light-as-air chiffon to crunchy, burlap-like tussah.

Silk, in an appropriate weight, can be substituted for rayon or cotton, and some of the heavier weaves can be substituted for wool or polyester fleece. To prepare silk fabrics for making fabric-yarn, iron the lighter weights with the correct iron setting. The heavier weights can be misted using a spray bottle filled with water, and hung to dry.

Wool

Wool is the shorn fleece of animals. Fleece can be obtained from many different animals, from sheep to yaks and from rabbits to dogs. The most popular wool, from sheep, can be dyed brilliant, highly saturated colors and woven into fabrics that range from light tropical weights to thick and spongy. The surface of wool can be enhanced by brushing or felting.

Wool is a fiber of choice for garments worn next to the body, with cashmere and pashmina the crème de la crème of the woolen family of fabrics. To prepare wool fabrics to be made into fabric-yarn, gently steam, steam iron, or mist with a spray bottle filled with water, and hang to dry.

Polyester and Nylon

Polyester and nylon fabrics are woven from man-made fibers. They come in a variety of weights and textures, ranging from organza, sheer, and lace to brushed polar fleece and faux fur. Although diverse, they all have one thing in common: polyester and nylon fabrics will melt if heated with too hot an iron.

Nylon and polyester fabrics can be substituted for most fabrics listed in the projects. These fabrics are great for projects being handled by children, as they are machine washable, nontoxic, and nonallergenic. To prepare polyester and nylon fabrics to be made into fabric-yarn, mist with a spray bottle filled with water, or tumble dry on low to remove the wrinkles.

Selvages

Selvages are the dense strips at the edges of woven or knit fabrics that prevent raveling.

Keeping the selvages or trimming them away prior to cutting fabric into fabric strips is a personal or design decision. In the case of printed fabrics, the selvage area is usually white, with the manufacturer's information printed along the edge. On yarn-dyed fabrics, the selvage is usually a tighter weave of the same yarns used in the body of the fabric, and may contain stronger synthetic yarns to help stabilize the goods during the weaving process.

Selvage edges

Painting, Dyeing, and Discharging

Painting, dyeing, and discharging are ways to add visual texture and dimension to your fabric prior to cutting the yardage into fabric strips for fabric-yarn. There are numerous fabric paints, dyes, and discharge products available in art, craft, and hobby stores. The methods I explain here were all used on 100% cotton quilting fabric. There are many other products and methods that can be used to alter the surface of the fabric, so use techniques that you are familiar with, or have fun exploring something new.

Always work with manageable pieces of fabric. I find that 1½- to 2-yard pieces are sizable enough for my liking, but you might need to process more fabric if specific lengths are required.

The cottons I used were misted with a spray bottle filled with water and ironed on the hottest setting to steam out the wrinkles prior to painting or discharging.

NOTE: As these are handcrafting techniques, your results will vary.

Painting and Dyeing

Always test a small piece of fabric before engaging in the bulk of the project. This helps determine whether your materials are compatible and allows you to get a feel for working with your technique.

Choose a paint or dye that is suitable for the fabric you have selected, and follow the manufacturer's instructions for its use.

Work in a well-lit, well-ventilated area, where creating a bit of a mess is not a problem.

Supplies

- 100% cotton fabric
- Fabric paint or dye of your choice (I used Pebeo Setacolor Transparent Paints for these examples)
- Eyedropper for spatter
- Bristle or foam brush for painting
- Protective gloves

Spatter

1. Fill an eyedropper with paint or dye. Slowly and carefully squeeze a single drop from the eye-dropper onto the fabric. First work in a circular motion across the fabric, and then in a grid pattern, manipulating drops to cover the surface of the fabric to your liking.
2. Allow the dye to set or the paint to dry according to the manufacturer's instructions. Heat set as needed by ironing on the wrong side of the fabric.

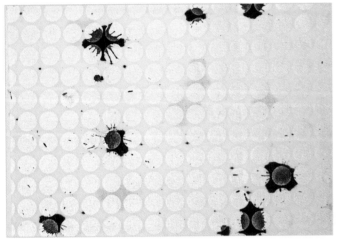

Ink spatter overdyeing is a perfect complement to metallic-pearl dot fabric.

Paint

1. Paint the color onto the right side of the fabric with a bristle or sponge brush. Diluted paint and dye produce a softer watercolor look with feathered edges. Nondiluted paint and dye produce solid color with very little bleeding.
2. Allow the dye to set or the paint to dry according to the manufacturer's instructions. Heat set as needed by ironing on the wrong side of the fabric.

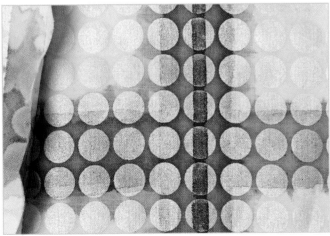

Painted fabric adds interest and texture.

Discharging

Discharging is the method of using bleach or a specially formulated product to remove color from the fabric. This technique, even more than dyeing, is unstructured and tends to be unpredictable but very fun. The best advice is to test a small sample of the fabric you want to discharge, and see if you like the results.

Different fabrics discharge differently, and many factors determine the outcome. All come into play in the end product. Bleach is applied to a fabric, and the fabric is placed in the sun. The bleach-saturated areas will fade and discharge color. Things to consider: Are you using 100% bleach, 50% bleach and 50% water, or some other combination of bleach and water? Is it a bright, sunny day or slightly overcast? Dark colors show better contrast than light colors do. Be assured that whatever circumstances prevail, your results will be unique for that piece of fabric.

NOTE: Avoid using chlorine bleach on any synthetic fiber; the damage is irreversible.

Supplies

- 100% cotton fabric for discharging
- Squeeze bottle with very narrow tip
- Bleach
- Hydrogen peroxide
- Bucket of warm, soapy water
- Protective gloves
- Plastic to protect work area (optional)

Discharge

NOTE: The conditions described below are an ideal scenario; adapt as needed to your particular situation.

TIP from Mark

If you don't have a squeeze bottle with a very narrow tip, here's a quick way to make one using a water bottle.

1. Unbend and straighten one end of a paper clip.
2. Heat the straightened end in the flame of a gas stove or a candle until it is glowing hot.
3. Gently touch the hot paper clip to the center of the water bottle cap and melt a small hole in the top.
4. Let the paper clip cool before discarding.

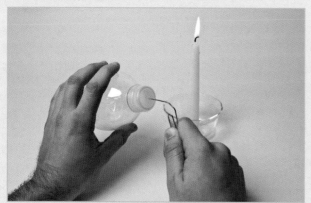

Make a squeeze bottle by piercing a hole in the cap.

1. Gather all the supplies in a centralized place, in a bright, sunny location.

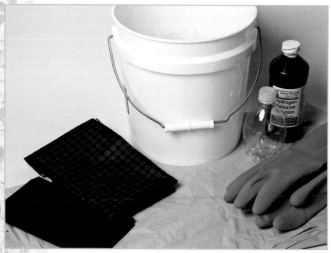

Supplies for discharging

2. Place the fabric right side up in the sun. If you're concerned about damaging your work area, protect the area with plastic.

3. In a bucket, mix 1 cup of hydrogen peroxide into 1 gallon of warm, soapy water.
4. Put on gloves and fill the squeeze bottle half-full with bleach. Then drip, squirt, squeeze, or dribble the bleach onto the fabric. When it has been covered sufficiently, stop. The sun and bleach will react immediately and lighten the color of the fabric.

Apply bleach to the fabric.

5. After the desired discharge effect or lightness has been achieved (after no more than 5 minutes), put on gloves, and plunge the fabric into the peroxide bath to neutralize the bleaching reaction. Soak for 20 minutes.
6. Rinse the fabric thoroughly in clean water. Machine wash the discharged piece of fabric with soap and liquid fabric softener on a gentle cycle.

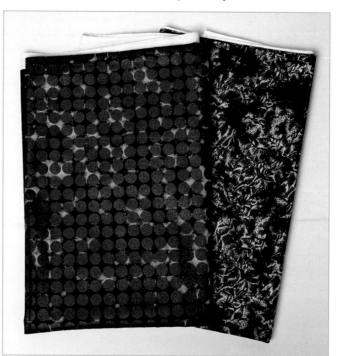

Discharged fabrics.

Ready, Set, Let's Start Strippin'

Cutting fabric into strips for fabric-yarn is one of the easiest things you can do. With a few simple tools you can create myriad different looks for all your fabric knitting projects. Think of all the fabrics you can use to make your own unique fabric-yarn.

There are many different types of fabrics you can start with (refer to pages 8–9). All the projects in this book include suggestions of appropriate fabrics to use. For example, cotton fabric is wonderful to work with and sturdy enough for a pillow, but it would be a bit weighty and rough for a hat. Felted wool, or cashmere, brings needed softness to a garment worn close to the head and over the ears.

Pillow made from cottons and linen

Fabric-Yarn

All the projects in this book were created with fabric-yarn made from strips cut on either the crosswise or lengthwise grain of the fabric. Fabric-yarn cut on the bias is too stretchy and can fall apart.

Fabric-yarn with frayed hairs

Almost all fabrics will feather or fray to varying degrees when cut and then knit. Some fabric frays create hairs similar to those of an eyelash yarn.

Strips that are ¼" wide are suitable for most projects and are easy to cut. They make a nice replication of twisted knitting yarn. You can also cut wider strips, which fold naturally while you are knitting. The pillow below was knit with a ⅜" fabric-yarn that folded in half during knitting, to create a thick-and-flat, thin-and-folded texture.

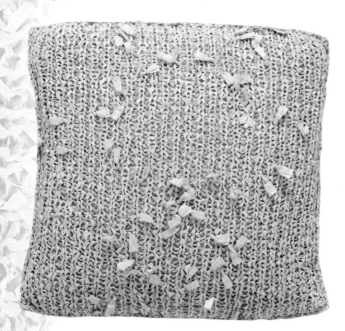

Pillow knit with ⅜" fabric-yarn

There are many ways to create fabric-yarn. It's a good idea to make a few strips, join them, and knit a test swatch before you prepare all your fabric-yarn. The following are some ideas to get you started.

Tearing Fabric Strips

Tearing fabric is the simplest and most basic approach to creating fabric strips. This works well with tightly woven fabrics such as cotton, rayon, and some synthetic sheers, but it can be tricky unless careful attention is paid to tearing the fabric in a particular manner. Test the method on your fabric to determine whether the weave is suitable for tearing.

Right-handers: work from left to right. Left-handers: work from right to left.

1. Place the fabric on a flat surface.
2. Make 1"-long snips through the fabric every ¼"–⅜". Looser-weave fabrics, such as sheers, may need wider strips.

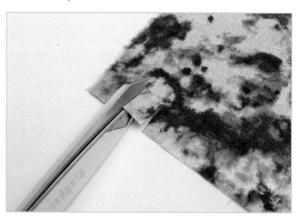

Snip the edge of the fabric.

3. Hold the piece of fabric in your left hand to stabilize it. With your right hand, firmly grasp the first little tag, made from snipping the fabric, between your thumb and forefinger.
4. Use a steady and determined motion to tear the fabric into a strip, pulling it toward the body of the fabric, or to the right. Pulling toward the fabric gives the strip more strength. If you pull away from the fabric, the strip will probably break or the fibers will just pull apart.

Pull.

Hold the fabric firmly and pull.

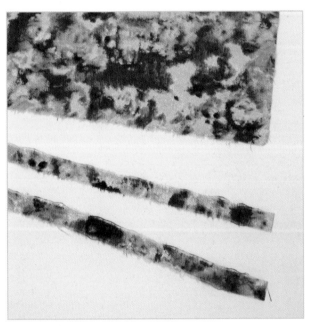

Tear the fabric into strips.

TIP
from Mark

If you like, you can keep the selvage edges on the fabric when you cut the strips. They can be used as a decorative component of the fabric-yarn.

Cutting Fabric Strips

Cutting Tools

There are a variety of tools you can use to cut your strips of fabric-yarn. Cutting may be a bit more time consuming than tearing, but it gives you more options and more control over the finished fabric-yarn. Your choice of tools depends on the fabric. I've provided some guidelines, but experiment as you see fit. For best results, cut your strips $\frac{1}{4}$" to $\frac{3}{8}$" wide.

Tools for cutting fabric strips

Scissors

Use conventional straight-edge scissors for the following tasks:

- Snipping the ends of fabric for tearing

- Cutting large open-weave fabrics between the threads

Scissors are available with a variety of decorative edges. However, for cutting fabric strips, it is easier and quicker to use a decorative blade in a rotary cutter or other cutting tool designed to make faster and easier work of the cutting process.

Knives and Blades

Craft knives, such as X-ACTO knives, or razor blades, make quick work of cutting knits such as faux fur and plush fabrics. Always work on top of a cutting mat to prevent damage to the work surface, and cut from the wrong side of the fabric.

Rotary Cutters

All fabrics can be cut with a regular rotary cutter, acrylic rotary ruler, and cutting mat. Moving a rotary ruler ¼″ after every cut seems a bit tedious, but it can be quite Zen. Once a rhythm and flow are achieved, the process becomes one continuous motion. Measure ¼″, hold down the ruler, cut the strip, and remove. Repeat. It's your mantra. Acrylic rulers with prespaced slots for cutting strips are also available.

Rotary cutters with decorative-edge blades are readily available and create pinked, ruffled, or wavy edges that are especially fun to use for fabric knitting.

Alto's QuiltCut2

Use a decorative blade for pinked, scalloped, or wavy edges.

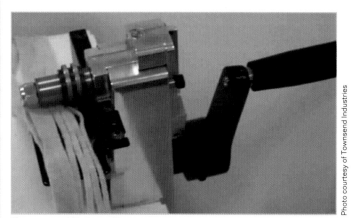

Townsend Fabric Cutter

Cutting Machines

Machines designed specifically for cutting lengths of fabric into strips are available. They are not inexpensive, but the investment will make cutting fabric strips easier and more fun. Two such devices are Alto's QuiltCut2 and the Townsend Fabric Cutter. The former is limited to thinner fabrics such as lightweight cotton, rayon, and silk that will fit under the locking bar, and the latter is designed for heavier fabrics such as wool and fleece.

For any machine, it's best to follow the manufacturer's guidelines, but some variation is possible. For example, the Townsend Fabric Cutter is designed for wools, but I found that it works nicely on polar fleece and sweatshirt material too.

 TIP from Mark

Don't be afraid to experiment. Some of my most interesting inspirations have come from using tools in ways other than they were originally intended to be used. Please be advised that when you use any tool in a manner other than what is recommended by the manufacturer, it is strictly at your own risk. But don't let that stop you. Go ahead. Be creative, but remember safety!

Continuous Fabric-Yarn

A continuous piece of fabric-yarn can be made by cutting fabric in a switchback design back and forth across the fabric. This works well with almost all fabrics and is the only method to produce faux fur fabric-yarn.

1. If you don't want the selvages in your fabric-yarn, remove them now.
2. Start at one side of the fabric and cut across to the opposite side, stopping ½"–⅝" from the edge.
3. Move the ruler the width of the fabric strip, and cut again. This time start cutting on the edge you stopped on last. Cut across the fabric strip, stopping ½"–⅝" from the opposite edge (the starting edge of the previous strip).
4. Repeat this process until the fabric is cut in a continuous accordion-like strip.

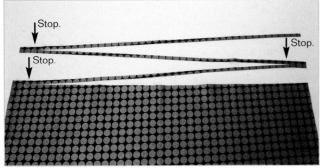

Stop ½"–⅝" from alternate edges to create a continuous strip.

Faux fur and plush knits are ideal fabrics for creating continuous fabric-yarn.

Work from the back of the fabric, and use a craft knife or razor blade to slit the fabric following a row of knit stitches. Be sure to cut in a lengthwise direction. Stop before the end of the fabric, and continue as explained at right.

Use craft knife to slit fabric.

TIP from Mark

If you don't want to cut your own fabric strips, you can buy precut fabric-yarn in all types of fibers. Refer to Resources on page 94 to find sources.

Precut fabric-yarn

Joining Fabric-Yarn Strips

There are numerous ways to join strips of fabric together into fabric-yarn. Most are quick and easy. Some work on specific types of fabrics, and some are just plain fun. Here are a few, but you may come up with a method that works better for you. Have fun experimenting.

 Use your own creative touch when making your fabric-yarn. Mix and match any of the stripping or joining techniques presented in any of the project instructions in this book to create a "uniquely you" heirloom.

Sewing

To sew fabric-yarn strips together, choose a thread that is compatible with your fabric and your project. Novelty threads are often the perfect addition, but considering the context of the design, a solid thread may be just what is needed.

Novelty threads for sewing fabric-yarn together

Continuous Sewing

One approach is to sew a continuous zigzag or hem stitch down the center of the fabric strips. This technique works best with thicker fabrics, such as wool. Join the ends of the fabric-yarn by overlapping the ends as you go along; backtack or stitch in place to reinforce the overlap and to add interest.

Sew a continuous stitch down the center of fabric strips.

 While making continuously sewn fabric-yarn, be creative. Feathers and other soft items can be stitched in while you are sewing the fabric strips together. The Tippi hat (page 80) has stitched-in feathers. Use pastel or white feathers to add a fantasy element to fabric-yarn for wedding, shower, or anniversary-themed projects.

Here's an easy method for simplifying the task of continuously sewing the fabric strips into fabric-yarn.

1. Overlap the ends of the fabric strips, and pin to hold them in place. Pin several lengths of fabric strips together at one time, but don't do too many at once. The pins might snag on the strips or your clothing and make a frustrating mess of the work.

Pin the fabric strips together.

2. Start to sew down the center of the first fabric strip. Hold the top and bobbin threads, and gently yet firmly guide the fabric strip under the presser foot. Once the machine is sewing smoothly and the fabric strip is being fed evenly, stop sewing with the needle down.

Hold the threads and guide the fabric under the presser foot.

3. Work the fabric strip in front of the needle into the open notch of the presser foot. Continue sewing. The notch acts as a guide and will keep the fabric strip flat and centered under the needle.

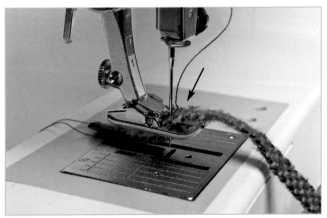

With the needle down, position the fabric strip in the notch of the presser foot.

4. Continue sewing with a steady and even motion. Slow down slightly when the pinned fabric-strip ends approach the presser foot. Work the fabric-strip end into the notch as you continue to sew, and remove the pin as you go.

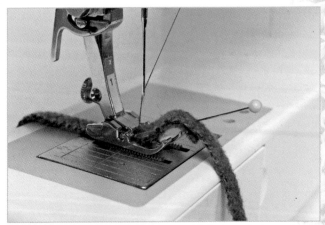

Slow down, and guide the pinned fabric strip into the presser foot notch.

5. For textural interest, I like to let the thread bunch up a bit to make slubs.

Thread buildup creates textural interest.

 TIP from Mark *With many stitch options to choose from, select a stitch that is compatible with the fabric and suits the style of the item you'll be knitting.*

Select a machine stitch appropriate to the fabric.

Sewing the Ends

Another method of joining together the fabric strips is to lap the ends, and stitch just the overlap. This technique works well with all fabric-yarn. At the point where the strips overlap, backtack or stitch in place to reinforce the overlap and to add surface interest. Pin a few overlapped ends at a time. Place the pinned ends under the presser foot, and lower it. Remove the pin, and sew.

Overlap the ends of the fabric strips, and stitch.

No-Sew Joining

Knotting

For thinner fabrics, simply tie knots to join the fabric strips together. An added benefit of this technique is that the knots provide decoration. When you tie knots in thicker fabric, you get larger, lumpier knots, which you can use to your advantage by embellishing them, adding another level of surface interest.

To tie knots, place the wrong sides of the fabric strips together, and join the ends by tying a knot.

1. Place the fabric strips wrong sides together.

2. Tie the fabric strips together.

3. Continue tying strips together to achieve the desired length of fabric-yarn.

> **TIP from Mark**
> *After looping the fabric strips to form a knot, pinch a length at the opposite end of the fabric strips, and secure the next knot at the desired length. This way all the tied ends are very close to the same length, making an attractive design detail.*

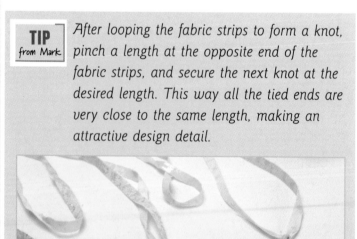

Leave a uniform-length tail when knotting to create unique design detail.

Adhesives

A quick way to join strips into fabric-yarn is to use glue. There are many glue choices to use on fabrics. I prefer Liquid Thread, a fabric adhesive that is heat set by ironing. To join fabric strips with glue, simply apply the adhesive to the overlapped ends, and attach them following the manufacturer's instructions. If recommended, heat set for a strong bond. Test your adhesive for strength and durability before using it on your fabric-yarn.

Glue the fabric strips together.

 TIP from Mark *Creating a production line is an easy way to make quick work out of gluing the fabric strips together.*

1. Place the fabric strips in pairs on an ironing board. One row will have the strips with the right sides facing up, and the other row will have their mates with the wrong sides facing up.
2. Apply the glue to the ends of the paired fabric strips, following the glue manufacturer's instructions. If necessary, allow the glue to dry. One set of strips will have the glue on the top side, and the other set will have the glue on the bottom.
3. Place the pairs of strips, glue sides together, and if necessary set the glue with a hot iron.
4. Continue gluing pairs of fabric strips. In turn, join the glued pairs of fabric strips together until all the fabric strips have been processed into a single ball of fabric-yarn.

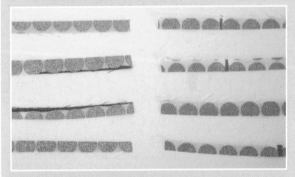

Arrange pairs of fabric strips for gluing.

Rhinestone Studs and Beads

Add sparkle to your fabric-yarn by using a rhinestone setter to join the fabric strips. Overlap the ends of the fabric strips over the rhinestone studding machine. Following the manufacturer's instructions, apply the rhinestone back, grasping the rhinestone and fabric strips together.

Decorative beads can also be added to fabric strips that have been sewn together.

Add beads for decoration.

Add rhinestones for sparkle.

Working the Fabric with Color

Don't hesitate to boldly mix colors and patterns in the fabrics you choose. They will be broken down into smaller bits of color and pattern that resemble the original fabric and become something more exotic. A perfect example of this is the transformation of the brushed wool plaid used in the Brushed Wool Throw with Alternating Cables and Bi-Colored Stripes (page 57). The plaid, when cut, fractured into a beautiful Donegal tweed–like fabric-yarn.

Fabric-yarn can be solid—one continuous length of the same color, pattern, and/or fabric.

Or, you can create color and pattern effects by joining together the individual fabric strips in a specific order. One effect is to shade the fabric-yarn from light to dark in a single color. You can also create patterns by using several different colors of fabrics and sewing them together in either a repeating or random order.

Solid-color fabric-yarns

Color-graded fabric-yarns

TIP from Mark *Tying on fabric-yarn strips as you knit allows you to follow your inspiration as you knit. Intermix different fabrics—cottons, wools, and rayons—for one-of-a-kind inspiration. This is a great way to use up extra strips and tails of fabric-yarn. And the result is something sophisticatedly bohemian!*

Storing the Cut Fabric Strips

As with any project, it is important to be organized. Anyone who works with fibers and fabrics knows that lint is an inherent part of working with such materials.

When fabrics are cut into fabric strips to make fabric-yarn, the lint factor is greatly increased. The lint can be contained if you process the fabric in a specific place and periodically vacuum the work area. Once the strips are cut, store them in a plastic zipper bag. All the lint will gather in the bag and can be easily discarded.

Winding the Fabric-Yarn into Balls of Fabric-Yarn

I like to wind the fabric-yarn into balls as I create it. This helps keep the continuous length of fabric-yarn more manageable. Store the finished balls in plastic zipper bags for organization and to minimize the spreading of lint.

Knitting Basics

This chapter outlines the basic knitting techniques and methods you'll need to complete the projects. The exciting news is that all knitting patterns consist of only two stitches, knit and purl. Master these stitches using the simple, easy-to-follow procedures in this chapter, and you will be on your way to creating one-of-a-kind knitted heirlooms to cherish and share with friends and loved ones.

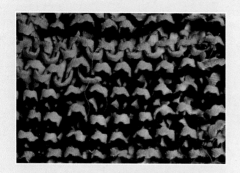

Basic Techniques

Slipknot

Everyone knows how to make a slipknot, but most of us don't realize it. It is as simple as making a loop with the fabric-yarn and pulling a second loop through the first one. Pull the opposite end to tighten the knot. Voilà!

Make a slipknot.

Cast On

Casting on is the starting point for all knitting. It is a simple procedure with many variations. I prefer the long-tail cast-on method, but use any method you are familiar with. Start with a tail of fabric-yarn that is long enough to cast on all your stitches. For cottons and thin fabrics, at least 1½″ of fabric-yarn for each stitch is needed; for heavier fabrics you'll need to allow more.

1. Measure out at least 1½″ of yarn for each stitch to be cast on. Make a slipknot, and wrap the yarn around your thumb and index finger as shown.

2. Insert the tip of the needle into the loop of fabric-yarn on your thumb. Wrap the tip of the needle behind the fabric-yarn on your index finger.

3. Pull the needle back through the loop on your thumb.

4. Pull the needle to tighten the loop.

Knit

Knit stitches are formed by pulling a loop of fabric-yarn through the stitch on the left knitting needle. The loop is pulled from the back of the work, toward you, finishing on the right needle. Knit stitches are easily identified because they form what looks like a V.

1. Insert the right needle into the loop of the next stitch from front to back.

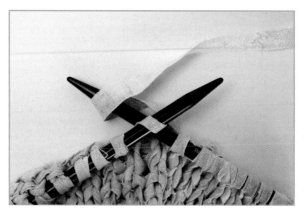

2. Bring the fabric-yarn over the right needle.

3. Pull the needle and fabric-yarn through the stitch.

4. Slide the stitch to the right needle.

Purl

Purl stitches are formed by pulling a loop of fabric-yarn through the stitch on the left knitting needle. The loop is pulled from the front of the work and back away from you, finishing on the right needle. Purl stitches are easily identified because they form dash-like bumps. Interesting thing—the reverse side of a knit stitch is a purl stitch, and vice versa.

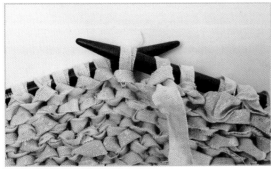

1. Insert the needle into the loop of the next stitch, keeping the yarn and needle in front.

2. Bring the yarn over the needle.

3. Pull the yarn through the stitch toward the back.

4. Slide the stitch to the right needle.

Stockinette or Jersey Stitch

The stockinette, or jersey, stitch combines knit and purl stitches to form a smooth knit surface on one side (stockinette) and a bumpy purl surface (reverse stockinette) on the other side.

Row 1 and All ODD Rows: Knit all stitches.
Row 2 and All EVEN Rows: Purl all stitches.
Continue the work by repeating Rows 1 and 2.

Stockinette: all knit stitches

Reverse stockinette: all purl stitches

Garter Stitch

The Garter stitch is what most beginning knitters master first, as all the rows are knit (no purling). Doing this forms rows of ridged stitches that resemble horizontal ribs.

All Rows: Knit all stitches.

1 × 1 and 2 × 2 Rib

A rib is a combination of knit and purl stitches that forms an accordion-like surface. Ribbing is very stretchy and is often used to form the bottoms, cuffs, and collars of sweaters.

1 x 1 RIB

In a 1 × 1 rib, one vertical row of knit stitches is followed by one vertical row of purl stitches. The knitting sequence will change based on an EVEN or ODD number of worked stitches.

Worked over an EVEN number of stitches

Row 1 and All Rows: *Knit 1 stitch, and Purl 1 stitch*. Repeat * to * across the remaining stitches, ending in a purl stitch.

Continue the work by repeating Row 1.

Worked over an ODD number of stitches

Row 1 and All ODD Rows: *Knit 1 stitch, and Purl 1 stitch*. Repeat * to * across the remaining stitches, ending in a knit stitch.

Row 2 and All EVEN Rows: *Purl 1 stitch, and Knit 1 stitch*. Repeat * to * across the remaining stitches, ending in a purl stitch.

Continue the work by repeating Rows 1 and 2.

2 x 2 RIB

A 2 × 2 rib expands the simple concept of a 1 × 1 rib and is normally worked over an EVEN number of stitches. Instead of one knit stitch followed by one purl stitch, two knit stitches are followed by two purl stitches.

Worked over multiples of 4 stitches

Row 1 and All Rows: *Knit 2 stitches, and Purl 2 stitches*. Repeat * to * across the remaining stitches, ending with 2 purl stitches.

Continue the work by repeating Row 1.

Moss or Seed Stitch

A moss or seed stitch is a simple alternating combination of knit and purl stitches that makes a very textured surface resembling moss or seeds.

Worked over ODD number of stitches

Row 1 and All Rows: *Knit 1 stitch, and Purl 1 stitch*. Repeat * to * across the remaining stitches, ending in a knit stitch.

Continue work by repeating Row 1.

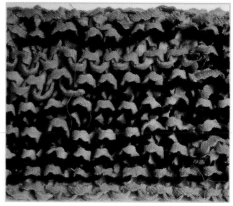

Garter stitch

1 × 1 rib

2 × 2 rib

Moss or seed stitch

Basketweave Stitch

The basketweave stitch is made up of alternating sets of knit and purl stitches. The resulting pattern forms textured blocks resembling woven caning.

Worked on multiples of 7 stitches

Row 1: * Knit 4 stitches, and Purl 3 stitches *. Repeat * to * across the remaining stitches, ending with 3 purl stitches.

Row 2: * Knit 3 stitches, and Purl 4 stitches *. Repeat * to * across the remaining stitches, ending with 4 purl stitches.

Rows 3 and 4: Repeat Rows 1 and 2.

Row 5: * Purl 4 stitches, and Knit 3 stitches *. Repeat * to * across the remaining stitches, ending with 3 knit stitches.

Row 6: * Purl 3 stitches, and Knit 4 stitches *. Repeat * to * across the remaining stitches, ending with 4 knit stitches.

Rows 7 and 8: Repeat Rows 5 and 6.

Continue the work by repeating Rows 1 through 8.

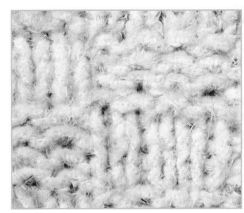

Basketweave stitch

Decrease

For shaped items such as The Tippi hat (page 80) or the Olivia Top (page 83), you will need to decrease. To do this, knit or purl 2 stitches together as 1.

Knit 2 together.

Purl 2 together.

Tie on Fabric-Yarn

Whether you've run out of fabric-yarn while knitting or need to make a color change, you'll need to add on to your project. Loosely tie the end of the new fabric-yarn to the end of the old fabric-yarn, leaving a tail about 4″ long. When your work is complete, pick apart the knot and weave in the ends (refer to page 33).

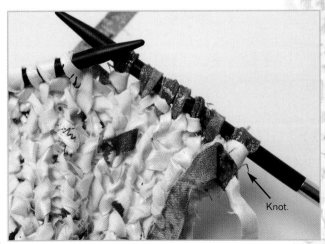

Knot.

Loosely tie the new fabric-yarn to the old.

Intarsia

Intarsia is used when knitting multiple colors in the same row to place color in specific areas. The design is visible from both the right and wrong sides of the work.

A simple example is the Multicolored Set Stripe Pillow (page 50). Intarsia is used in this project to place a different-colored vertical cable through the center of the pillow top.

Another example is The Perry—Zebra Stripe Intarsia Pillow (page 54). Here intarsia is used to create a zebra stripe pattern using many color changes within one row of knitting.

Intarsia cable from Multicolored Set Stripe Pillow

In order to produce a properly woven intarsia, without holes, you must cross the fabric-yarn when you make a color change. On the wrong side of the work, the fabric-yarn you just finished working *must* be placed on top of the fabric-yarn you are picking up. This practice crosses the fabric-yarn, thereby weaving the colors together.

Cast on the required number of stitches.

Row 1 (right side): Knit across the row, changing colors as directed by tying on new fabric-yarn to the fabric-yarn just worked (page 29).

Row 2 (wrong side): Purl across the row, changing colors as directed. As you pick up each color change, place the just-worked color on top, crossing the 2 strands of fabric-yarn in front of your work (wrong side).

Intarsia design from The Perry—Zebra Stripe Intarsia Pillow

Row 3 (right side): Knit across the required number of stitches, changing colors as directed. As you pick up each color change, place the just-worked color on top, crossing the 2 strands of fabric-yarn behind your work (wrong side).

Crossing fabric-yarn from the wrong (purl) side

Crossing fabric-yarn from the right (knit) side

Continue working the intarsia pattern, remembering to cross strands on the wrong side of your work whenever changing colors.

Cable

A cable is created when the order of the knit fabric-yarn stitches is switched. By changing the order, the fabric-yarn stitches crisscross to form the cable twist.

There are numerous combinations of twists that can create a multitude of different cables. The technique for a basic left-twisting cable, described below, will be used in the fabric-yarn projects in this book. Follow the specific instructions for the projects that include cables. You will need a cable or double-pointed needle to hold the transferred stitches during the cabling process.

The cable row will always be an ODD-numbered row, and on the right side of the work. The right side of the cable is always knit stitches.

In this example the cable is worked over 6 stitches.

Cable in the Brushed Wool Throw

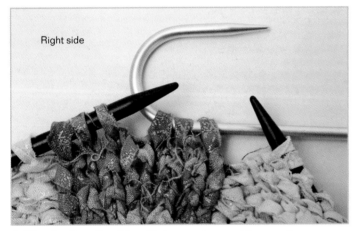

1. Slip the first 3 cable stitches onto a cable needle or double-pointed needle, and hold them to the wrong side, or the back, of the work.

2. Knit the next 3 stitches off the left knitting needle.

3. Knit the 3 stitches off the cable or double-pointed needle.

Gauge

Now that you know the stitches, it is a good time to discuss a very important part of accurate knitting: gauge. Gauge is calculated by knitting a small swatch and counting the number of stitches per inch. Since you are making your own fabric-yarn from your own selection of fabrics, it is highly likely that your gauges will vary from those suggested in this book. Because of this variability, each project's gauge is offered only as a *suggested* guideline.

The good news is that for most of the projects in this book, gauge isn't that important. The Simple 1 × 1 Rib Knit Pillow (page 45), Brushed Wool Throw (page 57), and Braided Illusion Scarf (page 77) are good examples. If your gauge differs from the project gauge, you'll still have an attractive finished project, albeit a bit smaller or larger. These projects give you great opportunities to experiment with different fabric-yarns.

The bad news is that for garments, gauge is extremely important. For example, if your gauge is off on the Olivia Top (page 83), your finished top may be better suited for the Abominable Snowman than for your petite sister, Twiggy.

Before starting a project and cutting yards of fabric, make a small quantity of fabric-yarn to check your gauge. If your gauge is way off, you may have to increase or reduce the width of your fabric strips or choose a different fabric. If your gauge is close to that suggested but still not exact, make adjustments in your needle size. Larger needles decrease the number of stitches per inch and smaller needles increase the number of stitches per inch. Blocking (page 34) can also help when a finished project is a little too small.

Before starting a project and cutting yards of fabric, make a small quantity of fabric-yarn to check your gauge.

Finishing Techniques

Bind Off

Binding off is the last step in knitting a project. It puts a finished edge (similar to the cast-on edge) on your work and keeps it from unraveling.

1. Knit 2 stitches onto your needle.
2. Use the left needle to lift the first stitch over the second stitch.

Take the first knit stitch and slip it over the second stitch.

There will be 1 stitch remaining on your right needle.

3. Knit another stitch. Repeat Step 2 until only 1 stitch remains.
4. Pull a long loop of fabric-yarn through the last stitch, as if to knit. Cut the loop and weave in the ends.

Weave in Fabric-Yarn Ends

After the knitting is completed and before the piece is blocked, the loose tail ends of fabric-yarn are woven into the stitches to conceal them. Use either a large-eye yarn needle or a crochet hook (your preference—either will achieve the same end result).

After you weave the ends, some may still peak through your work. If necessary, use a sewing needle and thread to stitch them into place so they don't show.

Weave the tail ends into the stitches.

Block

Blocking is the final step before the assembling or finishing of the project. In blocking, the knit piece is pinned to a board and misted with a spray bottle or steamed into the correct size and shape. When a finished project is slightly smaller than suggested, blocking is a good way to adjust it.

 TIP from Mark | *Simple and manageable blocking boards can be made out of ½″-thick foamcore board.*

1. Cut a piece of foamcore board to a size slightly bigger than the finished dimensions of the knitted project. In the instance of large or long projects, such as scarves and the Brushed Wool Throw, work in sections, and move the blocked area off the blocking board and reposition the remaining area as you go.

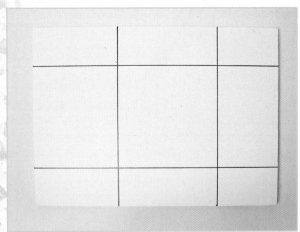

Cut foamcore board slightly bigger than the knit project. Mark the dimensions on the board.

2. Mark the finished dimensions on the surface of the board with a permanent marker or any writing tool that will not smudge and bleed when wet.

3. Pin the knit piece on the blocking board, easing it to the correct size.

4. With a spray bottle filled with water, or with a hand-held steamer, mist the pinned project. Allow the knit to dry and/or cool.

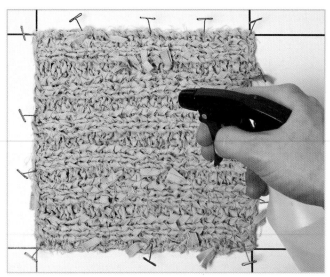

Pin the knit piece to the blocking board and mist with a spray bottle or steam.

5. Unpin the blocked piece from the foamcore board. Assemble the blocked pieces as directed.

Blocked piece

Fringe

Fringe can be added to a knitted piece for decoration or used to construct the piece, as in the Braided Illusion Scarf (page 77).

Braided Illusion Scarf with fringe

The single or multiple strands of fringe are tied onto the finished edges of the knitted piece.

1. Cut the strands of fringe twice the finished length and fold them in half.

Fold the fringe in half.

2. From the wrong side of the project (or from underneath), insert a crochet hook through a single set of stitches.
3. Hook the folded ends of one set of fringe, and pull it down through the stitches, forming a loop.

Insert a crochet hook into the edge stitch.

Pull a loop through the edge stitch.

4. Thread the cut ends of the fringe through the loop. Pull the loop tight.

Tighten the fringe loop.

5. Repeat Steps 2–4, adding fringe as required.

Pillow Backs

Mastering all the pillow backs is easy, as each variation is based on the one before it. Any pillow back is compatible with any knitted pillow front, so the various versions are interchangeable to help fuel your creativity. When making the pillow back, make certain the back measurements are adjusted to the finished and blocked size of the knitted pillow front, plus at least 1˝ on each side to accommodate the seam allowance and fabric variations.

Knitted Pillowcase

This is a pillow in its simplest form: two knit pieces sewn together and stuffed.

Sew through knit stitches.

Materials

- 2 blocked knit pieces of equal size, for pillow front and back
- Large-eyed yarn needle
- Matching perle cotton embroidery thread
- Pillow form (1″ larger on each side than finished pillow top)

Assembly

1. Align the blocked front and back, wrong sides together. Use a yarn needle and matching embroidery thread to sew back and forth through the knit stitches, catching one complete stitch each time the needle passes through the layers. Sew 3 sides together.

2. Stuff the pillow form into the open pillowcase. Sew the last side of the pillow closed in the same manner as the other sides.

Envelope Back

This pillow back has two pieces that overlap for the closure. You can make them from one fabric or piece together strips.

Envelope back

Materials

| BLOCKED KNIT PILLOW FRONT | BACKING PANELS (choose one option) | | LINING | BATTING (FUSIBLE) | PILLOW FORM |
	SOLID PILLOW BACK	STRIPED PILLOW BACK			
16″ × 16″	2 @ 18″ × 14$\frac{1}{2}$″	10 @ 18″ × 3$\frac{3}{4}$″	2 @ 18″ × 14$\frac{1}{2}$″	2 @ 18″ × 14″	18″ × 18″
18″ × 18″	2 @ 20″ × 15$\frac{1}{2}$″	10 @ 20″ × 3$\frac{7}{8}$″	2 @ 20″ × 15$\frac{1}{2}$″	2 @ 20″ × 15″	20″ × 20″

Additional materials: Sewing thread and hand-sewing needle

TIP from Mark

STRIPED PILLOW BACK

For a striped pillow back, use a ½″ seam allowance, and sew backing strips together lengthwise, creating 2 sets of equal numbers of strips. Each strip set will be one flap of the envelope pillow back.

Assembly

1. Align one long side of each pillow back panel (solid or striped) with a lining rectangle, right sides together. Pin. Using a ½″ seam allowance, sew along the aligned edge. Press the seams open.

2. Fold the pillow back and lining layers wrong sides together. Press.

3. If you don't want to quilt the pillow back, proceed to Step 5.

   Insert a batting piece between the layers of each of the pillow back panels. Position the batting with a long side against the stitched seam, fusible side facing the wrong (lining) side of the pillow back. Fuse the batting to the pillow back, following the manufacturer's instructions.

 I like using fusible batting because you can iron it in place and quilt without pinning. Use the batting of your choice for the pillow backs.

4. On the right side of the pillow back panels, quilt the layers together. For a striped pillow back, stitch over the seams with a zigzag stitch. For a solid pillow back, stitch lines with a straight or novelty stitch every 2½".

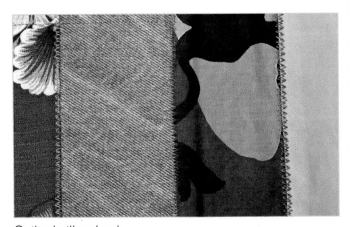

Quilted pillow back

5. Place the layered pillow back panels on the work surface in front of you, lining side down and the seamed sides facing each other. Overlap the 2 pieces, right over left, 5". Measure again to make sure the overlapped pieces make a single back piece that is 1" larger on all sides than the blocked knit pillow front. Trim to size if necessary. Pin the overlapped portion. Baste around the outside of the overlapped back piece ¼" away from the raw edge.

6. Press a ½" seam allowance to the wrong side of the pillow back (lining side) around all 4 edges. Pin, and baste close to the raw turned edge. On the right side, sew all around the pillow back, just shy of ½", following the basting stitch. I like to use a zigzag or other decorative stitch.

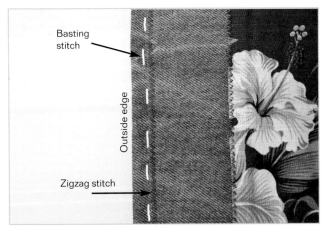

Sew around the outside edge with a straight or decorative stitch.

7. With wrong sides together and using 2 strands of thread, hand sew the envelope pillow back to the knit pillow front. Sew just inside the last row of knit stitches, catching both the fabric-yarn and the turned seam allowance of the pillow back. Be careful not to go all the way through to the right side of the pillow back.

Sew the knit front to the fabric back.

8. Open the flaps of the envelope pillow back, and stuff the pillow form into the pillowcase.

Faux and Functional Button Back

The faux or functional button back is constructed in the same way as the envelope back, with two changes. For a faux button closure, the buttons are sewn onto the pillow back after the two back panels are joined together. If functional buttonholes are desired, they are made before the two back panels are joined together.

Faux button back

Materials

BLOCKED KNIT PILLOW FRONT	BACKING PANELS (choose one option)		LINING	BATTING (FUSIBLE)	PILLOW FORM
	SOLID PILLOW BACK	STRIPED PILLOW BACK*			
16″ × 16″	2 @ 18″ × 12″	10 @ 18″ × 3¼″	2 @ 18″ × 12″	2 @ 17″ × 11½″	18″ × 18″
18″ × 18″	2 @ 20″ × 13″	10 @ 20″ × 3⅜″	2 @ 20″ × 13″	2 @ 20″ × 12½″	20″ × 20″

*Refer to Striped Pillow Back (page 38) for piecing instructions.
Additional materials: Decorative buttons, sewing thread, and hand-sewing needle

Faux Button Back Assembly

1. Construct the envelope back through Step 4 (pages 38–39). Skip Steps 3 and 4 if you don't want a quilted back.

2. Place the layered pillow back panels on the work surface in front of you, lining side down and the seamed sides facing each other. Overlap the 2 pieces, right over left, 2½″. Measure again to make sure the overlapped panels make a single back piece that is 1″ larger on all sides than the blocked knit

pillow front. Trim to size if necessary. Pin the over-lapped portion. Baste around the outside of the overlapped back piece ¼″ away from the raw edge.

3. Press a ½″ seam allowance to the wrong side of the pillow back (lining side) around all 4 edges. Pin, and baste close to the raw turned edge. On the right side, sew all around the pillow back, just shy of ½″, following the basting stitch.

Overlap the pillow back pieces 2½″, and sew the outside edges.

4. Sew buttons onto the face of the pillow back through both pillow back halves.

5. With wrong sides together and using 2 strands of thread, hand sew the faux button pillow back to the knit pillow front. Sew just inside the last row of knit stitches, catching both the fabric-yarn and the turned seam allowance of the pillow back. Be careful not to go all the way through to the right side of the pillow back. Sew 3 sides of the pillow.

6. Stuff the pillow form into the pillowcase through the open side, then sew the last side closed.

Functional Button Back Assembly

1. Construct the envelope back through Step 4 (pages 38–39). Skip Steps 3 and 4 if you don't want a quilted back.

2. On the seamed side of the right pillow back panel, mark buttonholes parallel to and ½″ away from the seamed edge. Make buttonholes on a machine or by hand. Cut open.

3. Place the layered pillow back panels on the work surface in front of you, lining side down and the seamed sides facing each other. Overlap the 2 back panels, right (buttonhole side) over left, 2½″. Mark the button placement on the left half.

4. Sew the buttons onto the left side, aligning the buttons with the buttonholes. Button the back closed.

Align the buttons with the buttonholes.

5. Measure again to make sure the overlapped pieces make a single back piece that is 1″ larger than the blocked knit pillow front. Trim to size if necessary. Pin the overlapped portion. Baste around the outside of the overlapped back piece ½″ away from the raw edge.

6. Press a ½″ seam allowance to the wrong side of the pillow back (lining side) around all 4 sides. Pin, and baste close to the raw turned edge. On the right side, sew all around the pillow back, just shy of ½″, following the basting stitch.

7. With wrong sides together and using 2 strands of thread, hand sew the functional button pillow back to the knit pillow front. Sew just inside the last row of knit stitches, catching both the fabric-yarn and the turned seam allowance of the pillow back. Be careful not to go all the way through to the right side of the pillow back. Sew all 4 sides of the pillow.

8. Open the back button closure and insert the pillow form. Rebutton the pillowcase.

Zipper Back

This no-fuss way to install a zipper is decorative as well as almost foolproof.

Materials

| BLOCKED KNIT PILLOW FRONT | BACKING PANELS (choose one option) | | LINING | ZIPPER EXTENSION (USE BACKING FABRIC) | ZIPPER | BATTING (FUSIBLE) | PILLOW FORM |
	SOLID PILLOW BACK	STRIPED PILLOW BACK*					
16″ × 16″	2 @ 18″ × 9½″	8 @ 18″ × 3⅛″	2 @ 18″ × 9½″	1 @ 3½″ × 9″	14″	2 @ 18″ × 9″	18″ × 18″
18″ × 18″	2 @ 20″ × 10½″	8 @ 20″ × 3⅜″	2 @ 20″ × 10½″	1 @ 3½″ × 9″	16″	2 @ 20″ × 10″	20″ × 20″

*Refer to Striped Pillow Back (page 38) for piecing instructions.
Additional materials: Sewing thread and hand-sewing needle

Zipper Extensions

1. Cut the 3½″ × 9″ zipper extension fabric in half crosswise, creating 2 extensions 3½″ × 4½″.

2. Center the long side of one fabric extension on the zipper tape, right sides together and edges even. Pin in place. Repeat for the other side.

3. Sew the zipper tape and fabric together using a ½″ seam. Press the fabric extensions away from the zipper.

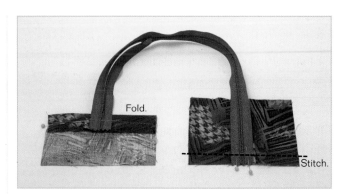

Sew the extension to the zipper.

Assembly

1. With right sides together, align and pin a long edge of one pillow back panel (solid or striped) to the zipper tape and extension as shown. Sew using a ½″ seam. Repeat to attach the zipper to the other pillow back panel. Trim excess fabric from the extension. Press the pillow back seam and zipper tape away from the zipper.

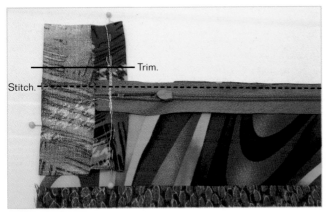

Align, pin, and sew the pillow back panels to the zipper and extensions.

2. Baste around the zipper tape through all layers of the seam, securing the seam in place on the wrong side of the panel.

Edgestitch around the zipper, and quilt if desired.

3. Press under a ½″ seam allowance along one long edge of each lining rectangle. With the wrong sides together, overlap the pressed edge of the lining fabric over the zipper tape and basting stitches, sandwiching the raw edges and seams between the pieces but not covering the zipper teeth. Baste all the layers together. Edgestitch around the zipper on the right side of the fabric.

4. If you don't want to quilt the pillow back, proceed to Step 6.

Insert a batting piece between the layers of each of the pillow back panels, fusible side facing the wrong (lining) side of the pillow back. Align the edge of the batting with the zipper tape and make certain the ends touch but do not overlap the zipper tape.

Fuse the batting to the pillow back, following the manufacturer's instructions.

5. On the right side of the pillow back, quilt the layers together. For a striped pillow back, stitch over the seams with a straight or zigzag stitch. For a solid pillow back, stitch lines with a straight or novelty stitch every 2½″.

6. Close the zipper and measure to make sure the zippered pillow back is 1″ larger on all sides than the blocked knit pillow front. Trim to size if necessary.

7. Press a ½″ seam allowance to the wrong side (lining side) of the zippered pillow back around all 4 sides. Pin, and baste close to the raw turned edge. On the right side, sew all around the pillow back, just shy of ½″ and following the basting stitches.

Sew around the pillow following the basting stitches.

8. With wrong sides together and using 2 strands of thread, hand sew the zipper pillow back to the knit pillow front. Sew just inside the last row of knit stitches, catching both the fabric-yarn and the turned seam allowance of the pillow back. Be careful not to go all the way through to the right side of the pillow back.

Sew the knit front to the fabric back.

 TIP *from Mark* — *Open the zipper and insert your hand into the pillowcase when sewing the front to the back.*

9. Open the zipper and stuff the pillowcase with the pillow form.

Home Decor

Simple 1 x 1 Rib Knit Pillow
with or without Knots

Finished size: 16″ × 16″

This pillow combines the simplest elements of knitting with fabric: fabric-yarn made from 100% cotton quilting fabric, strips cut with straight edges, and tied ends. The knots can be worked to the face as understated decoration, or to the back for a clean ribbed surface to embellish. And then sometimes, by pure chance, other variations magically emerge.

The crispness of quilting cotton and its timeless durability make it a perfect and easily accessible fabric of choice for this project. A metallic or pearl finish adds depth to the simplicity of cotton.

What You'll Need

NEEDLES/GAUGE

Gauge (refer to page 32): 11 stitches per 3″. Try size 9 needles, and adjust as needed.

FABRIC

Your yardage requirements may vary. Refer to Woven Fabric versus Knit Fabric (page 7) and Fabric-Yarn (page 14).

Fabric-Yarn: 2¼ yards 100% cotton quilting fabric, 44″–45″ wide

For each 16″ × 16″ pillow front or back, you will need 120 yards of fabric-yarn; 2¼ yards makes enough fabric-yarn for a knitted front and back.

Fabric options for Simple 1 × 1 Rib Knit Pillow—with or without Knots

NOTIONS

- Rotary cutter, ruler, and mat
- Large-eye yarn needle
- Medium crochet hook (optional)
- Sewing needle
- Sewing thread to match fabric
- 1 skein perle cotton or mercerized embroidery thread to match your fabric
- 18″ × 18″ pillow form

Preparation

Refer to Ready, Set, Let's Start Strippin' (pages 13–23).

Fabric-Yarn: Use a rotary cutter and a ruler to cut the fabric lengthwise into ⅜″ strips. Tie the ends together, and wind into several balls of fabric-yarn.

Knitting

Instructions are for 1 pillow front or back. Make 2 (1 for each side of the pillow).

The pillow is worked in 1 × 1 rib stitch (page 28) over an EVEN number of stitches. When worked over an EVEN number of stitches, the 1 × 1 rib is the same on either side of the finished piece.

CAST ON

Loosely cast on 58 stitches.

ROW 1 AND ALL ROWS

Knit 1 stitch, and Purl 1 stitch. Repeat * to * across the remaining stitches, and end with a purl stitch.

CONTINUE KNITTING

Repeat Row 1 until the piece measures 16″ × 16″.

As you knit, work the knots to either the front or the back of the piece, depending on your preference.

Working knots to the back of the piece results in a clean look.

When working knots to the front, different patterns emerge.

Finishing

Refer to pages 33–35.

1. Loosely bind off (page 33) all the stitches.

2. Use a large-eye needle or crochet hook to weave the loose tail ends of the fabric-yarn into the body of the work or along the finished edges.

3. If necessary, hide the ends of the fabric-yarn by using a sewing needle and thread to stitch them so they don't show.

4. Block (page 34) the finished front and back so they measure 16″ × 16″ each.

5. Use the knitted pillowcase method (page 37) to finish the pillow.

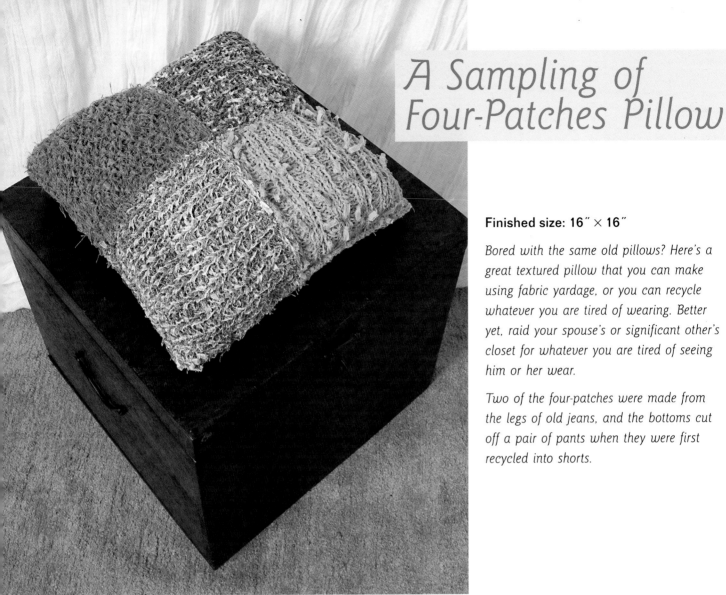

A Sampling of Four-Patches Pillow

Finished size: 16″ × 16″

Bored with the same old pillows? Here's a great textured pillow that you can make using fabric yardage, or you can recycle whatever you are tired of wearing. Better yet, raid your spouse's or significant other's closet for whatever you are tired of seeing him or her wear.

Two of the four-patches were made from the legs of old jeans, and the bottoms cut off a pair of pants when they were first recycled into shorts.

What You'll Need

NEEDLES/GAUGE

Gauge (refer to page 32): 5 stitches per 2″. Try size 9 needles, and adjust as needed for each fabric-yarn.

FABRICS

Your yardage requirements may vary. Refer to Woven Fabric versus Knit Fabric (page 7) and Fabric-Yarn (page 14).

Fabric-Yarn

Fabric A: ½ yard Hawaiian-print 100% cotton bark-cloth, 44″–45″ wide, or the equivalent, for 80 yards of fabric-yarn

Fabric B: ½ yard 100% cotton khaki fabric, 58″ wide, or the equivalent, for 45 yards of fabric-yarn

Fabric C: ½ yard linen or linen-like fabric, 48″–50″ wide (I used the front and back bottom portions of ramie/cotton pants cut open at the inner seam, with the outer seam left intact), or the equivalent, for 45 yards of fabric-yarn

Fabric D: ½ yard cotton denim, 44″–45″ wide (I used the front and back leg sections of 2 pairs of worn but not holey jeans, saving 1 panel for the back of the pillow), or the equivalent, for 80 yards of fabric-yarn

Pillow Back and Lining

Choose either the striped or solid pillow back option (refer to page 38).

    Option 1 – Striped Pillow Back: ¼ yard additional from each of fabrics A, B, C, and D.

    Option 2 – Solid Pillow Back: ½ yard 100% cotton quilting fabric, 44″–45″ wide; use a coordinating fabric or an additional ½ yard of any fabric-yarn fabric

    Lining: ½ yard 100% cotton quilting fabric, 44″–45″ wide

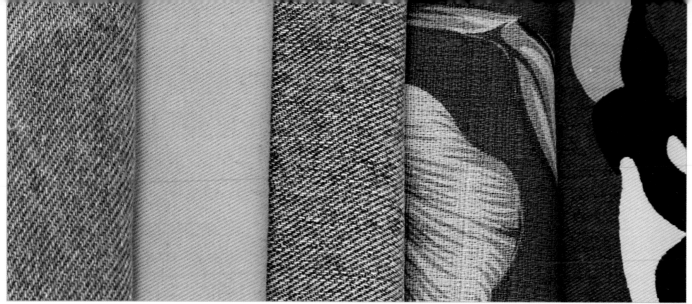

Fabric options for A Sampling of Four-Patches Pillow

NOTIONS

- Rotary cutter, ruler, and mat
- Large-eye yarn needle
- Medium crochet hook (optional)
- Sewing needles
- Sewing thread to match fabrics
- 1 skein perle cotton or mercerized embroidery thread to match your patches
- 20″ × 30″ batting (optional)
- 18″ × 18″ pillow form

Preparation

Refer to Ready, Set, Let's Start Strippin' (pages 13–23).

Fabric-Yarn A: Use a rotary cutter and a ruler to cut the fabric crosswise into ¼″ strips. Use a continuous stitch to join the fabric strips together. Backtack the lapped ends, and wind into 1 ball of fabric-yarn.

Fabric-Yarn B: Use a rotary cutter and a ruler to cut the fabric crosswise into ⅜″ strips. Tie the ends together, and wind into 1 ball of fabric-yarn.

Fabric-Yarn C: Use a rotary cutter and a ruler to cut the fabric crosswise into ⅜″ strips. Use a continuous stitch to join the fabric strips together. Backtack the lapped ends, and wind into 1 ball of fabric-yarn.

Fabric-Yarn D: Use a rotary cutter and a ruler to cut the fabric crosswise into ¼″ strips. Use a continuous stitch to join the fabric strips together. Backtack the lapped ends, and wind into 1 ball of fabric-yarn.

Knitting

Knit each of the 4 patches tightly, so they can be blocked to size, and the constant tension of the pillow insert will not cause gaps in the knit.

 TIP from Mark *A quick way to see if your knit patch is long enough is to fold it diagonally. When one side is as long as the cast-on edge, you have a square.*

Fold the patch diagonally to check progress.

CAST ON AND KNIT – BLOCK A

Fabric-Yarn A: Loosely cast on 23 stitches.

Work in a 1 × 1 rib over an ODD number of stitches (page 28):

> **Row 1 and All ODD Rows:** Begin and end with a knit stitch.

> **Row 2 and All EVEN Rows:** Begin and end with a purl stitch.

> Repeat Rows 1 and 2 until the block is square (refer to tip on page 48). Loosely bind off the last row (page 33).

CAST ON AND KNIT – BLOCK B

Fabric-Yarn B: Cast on 26 stitches.

Work in a 2 × 2 rib (page 28):

> **Row 1 and All ODD Rows:** * Knit 2 stitches, and Purl 2 stitches*. Repeat * to * across the remaining stitches, ending with 2 knit stitches.

> **Row 2 and All EVEN Rows:** * Purl 2 stitches, and Knit 2 stitches*. Repeat * to * across the remaining stitches, ending with 2 purl stitches.

> Work the knots to the front (ODD-row side). Repeat Rows 1 and 2 until the block is square. Loosely bind off the last row.

CAST ON AND KNIT – BLOCK C

Fabric-Yarn C: Loosely cast on 20 stitches.

Work in moss stitch (page 28) until the block is square. Loosely bind off the last row.

CAST ON AND KNIT – BLOCK D

Fabric-Yarn D: Cast on 23 stitches.

Repeat the instructions for Block A.

Finishing

Refer to pages 33–35.

1. Use a large-eye needle or crochet hook to weave the loose tail ends of the fabric-yarn into the body of the finished block or along the finished edges.

2. If necessary, hide the ends of the fabric-yarn by using a sewing needle and thread to stitch them so they don't show.

3. Block (page 34) each patch so it measures 9″ × 9″.

4. Lay out the 4 finished patches, right sides facing up.

5. Sew pairs of patches wrong sides together: A to B and C to D. Use the large-eye needle and perle cotton embroidery thread to sew back and forth through the knit stitches, catching one complete stitch each time the needle passes. Tie the ends of the embroidery thread, then weave the ends through the knit on the wrong side of the patches to hide them. The seams are on the right side of the patches and are used decoratively.

Sew the patches together.

6. Join the 2 halves, wrong sides together: A/B to C/D. Sew them together as you did for the pairs of patches above.

7. Block the pieced knit pillow top to make a 16″ × 16″ square and straighten the seams.

8. Use the envelope back method (pages 38–39), or any other pillow back method, to finish the pillow.

Multicolored Set Stripe Pillow
with Centered Intarsia Cable

Finished size: 18″ × 18″

Intarsia is the method of placing color in a specific area as you knit. Here the color is changed in each row for the inset placement of an intarsia cable that is a different color. This is another fun and simple project that has a few design elements working together at the same time.

The easy workability of cotton is preferred for this project. In addition, the fabrics have been processed with bleach (pages 11–12) or are recycled worn garments that have been laundered to a soft perfection.

What You'll Need

NEEDLES/GAUGE

Gauge (refer to page 32): 13 stitches per 3½″. Try size 9 needles, and adjust as needed.

FABRICS

Your yardage requirements may vary. Refer to Woven Fabric versus Knit Fabric (page 7) and Fabric-Yarn (page 14).

Fabric-Yarn

Fabric A: ⅝ yard 100% cotton quilting fabric, 44″–45″ wide, or the equivalent, for 90 yards of fabric-yarn

Fabric B (center cable): ⅝ yard 100% cotton quilting fabric, 44″–45″ wide, or the equivalent, for 45 yards of fabric-yarn

Fabric C: ⅜ yard 100% cotton pinwale corduroy, 44″–45″ wide, or the equivalent, for 45 yards of fabric-yarn

Fabric D: ⅝ yard 100% cotton quilting fabric, 44″–45″ wide (I used a combination of several fabrics), or the equivalent, for 90 yards of fabric-yarn

Fabric E: ¼ yard 100% cotton quilting fabric, 44″–45″ wide, to coordinate with fabric G, or the equivalent, for 45 yards of fabric-yarn (Fabric-yarns E and G will be combined when knit.)

Fabric F: ½ yard 100% cotton quilting fabric, 44″–45″ wide, or the equivalent, for 45 yards of fabric-yarn

Fabric G: ¼ yard polyester fleece fabric, 58″ wide, to coordinate with fabric E, or the equivalent, for 45 yards of fabric-yarn (Fabric-yarns E and G will be combined when knit.)

Pillow Back and Lining

Choose either the striped or solid faux button pillow back option (refer to page 40).

Option 1 – Striped Pillow Back: ¼ yard additional from each of fabrics A, C, D, E, and F

Option 2 – Solid Pillow Back: ½ yard 100% cotton quilting fabric, 44″–45″ wide; use a coordinating fabric or an additional ½ yard of any fabric-yarn fabric

Lining: ½ yard 100% cotton quilting fabric, 44″–45″ wide

NOTIONS

- Rotary cutter, ruler, and mat
- Decorative-edge rotary blade
- Fabric glue
- Beads (optional)
- Large cable needle
- Large-eye yarn needle
- Medium crochet hook (optional)
- Sewing needle
- Sewing thread to match fabrics
- 20″ × 20″ batting (optional)
- 20″ × 20″ pillow form
- 7 large buttons (optional for button or faux button back)

Preparation

Refer to Ready, Set, Let's Start Strippin' (pages 13–23).

Fabric-Yarn A: Use a rotary cutter and a ruler to cut the fabric crosswise into ¼″ strips. Glue the fabric strips together, and wind into 2 balls of fabric-yarn that are about the same size.

Fabric-Yarn B: Use a rotary cutter and a ruler to cut the fabric crosswise into ⅜″ strips. Tie the ends together, and wind into 1 ball of fabric-yarn.

Fabric-Yarn C: Use a rotary cutter and a ruler to cut the fabric crosswise into ¼″ strips. Glue the fabric strips together, and wind into 2 balls of fabric-yarn that are about the same size.

Fabric-Yarn D: Use a rotary cutter fit with a decorative blade to cut the fabric crosswise into ¼″ strips. Glue, hand bead, and/or backtack the fabric strips together. Wind into 2 balls of fabric-yarn that are about the same size.

Fabric-Yarn E: Use a rotary cutter and a ruler to cut the fabric crosswise into ⅛″ strips. Glue the fabric strips together, and wind into 2 balls of fabric-yarn that are about the same size.

Fabric-Yarn F: Snip the selvage edges of the fabric into ¼″–⅜″ tabs. Tear the fabric crosswise into strips. Tie the ends together, and wind into 2 balls of fabric-yarn that are about the same size.

Fabric-Yarn G: Use a rotary cutter and a ruler to cut the fabric crosswise into ¼″ strips. Tie the ends together, and wind into 2 balls of fabric-yarn that are about the same size.

Fabric options for Multicolored Set Stripe Pillow with Centered Intarsia Cable

Knitting

Refer to page 30 for intarsia knitting.

The color changes are worked over 12 rows, with the intarsia cable cross in the middle of each color block. You'll use 3 balls of fabric-yarn per row (2 balls for the background color and 1 for the intarsia cable). ODD rows are the right side of the work; EVEN rows are the wrong side. Striped knitting is worked in a 1 × 1 rib (page 28).

The cable is worked over 10 stitches.

CAST ON

Fabric-Yarn A: Loosely cast on 62 stitches.

ROW 1

Fabric-Yarn A: *Knit 1 stitch, and Purl 1 stitch*. Repeat * to * 12 more times, for a total of 26 stitches.
Fabric-Yarn B: Tie on the ball of fabric-yarn B. Knit 10 stitches.
Fabric-Yarn A: Tie on the second ball of fabric-yarn A. Purl 1 stitch, and Knit 1 stitch to the end of the row (26 stitches).

ROW 2

Fabric-Yarn A: *Purl 1 stitch, and Knit 1 stitch*. Repeat * to * 12 more times (26 stitches).
Fabric-Yarn B: Pick up fabric-yarn B. Cross fabric-yarn A on top of fabric-yarn B on the wrong side (see page 30). Purl 10 stitches. Work the knots to the wrong side.
Fabric-Yarn A: Pick up fabric-yarn A. Cross fabric-yarn B on top of fabric-yarn A. Knit 1 stitch, and Purl 1 stitch to the end of the row (26 stitches).

ROW 3

Fabric-Yarn A: *Knit 1 stitch, and Purl 1 stitch*. Repeat * to * 12 more times, for a total of 26 stitches.
Fabric-Yarn B: Pick up fabric-yarn B. Cross fabric-yarn A on top of fabric-yarn B on the wrong side of the work. Knit 10 stitches.
Fabric-Yarn A: Pick up fabric-yarn A. Cross fabric-yarn B on top of fabric-yarn A. Purl 1 stitch, and Knit 1 stitch to the end of the row (26 stitches).

ROWS 4 AND 6

Repeat Row 2.

ROW 5

Repeat Row 3.

ROW 7 – CABLE ROW

Fabric-Yarn A: *Knit 1 stitch, and Purl 1 stitch*. Repeat * to * 12 more times, for a total of 26 stitches.
Fabric-Yarn B: Work the cable over the next 10 stitches (refer to page 31): *Place the first 5 stitches of fabric-yarn B on a cable needle to the back of the work. Cross fabric-yarn A on top of fabric-yarn B. Knit 5 stitches off the knitting needle. Knit the 5 stitches off the cable needle.*
Fabric-Yarn A: Pick up fabric-yarn A. Cross fabric-yarn B on top of fabric-yarn A. Purl 1 stitch, and Knit 1 stitch to the end of the row (26 stitches).

ROWS 8, 10, AND 12

Repeat Row 2.

ROWS 9 AND 11

Repeat Row 3.

CONTINUE KNITTING

Repeat Rows 1–12 as follows to complete the pillow top:

 TIP from Mark *Master Rows 1-12, then use the illustration on page 53 as a quick reference for repeating each of the seven color changes.*

Rows 13–24

Repeat Rows 1–12, substituting fabric-yarn C for fabric-yarn A.

Rows 25–36

Repeat Rows 1–12, substituting fabric-yarn D for fabric-yarn A.

Rows 37–48

Repeat Rows 1–12, using fabric-yarn A.

Rows 49–60

Repeat Rows 1–12, substituting fabric-yarn D for fabric-yarn A.

Rows 61–72

Repeat Rows 1–12, substituting fabric-yarn E and G worked together as 1 strand in place of fabric-yarn A.

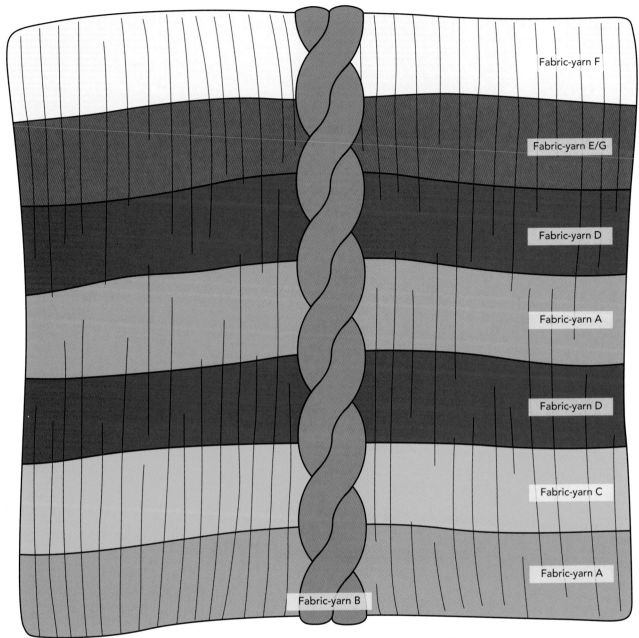

Multicolored Set Stripe Pillow color and cable changes

Rows 73–84

Repeat Rows 1–12, substituting fabric-yarn F for fabric-yarn A.

Finishing

Refer to pages 33–35.

1. Using fabric-yarn F, loosely bind off (page 33) all the stitches.
2. Use a large-eye needle or crochet hook to weave the loose tail ends of the fabric-yarn into the body of the work or along the finished edges.
3. If necessary, hide the ends of the fabric-yarn by using a sewing needle and thread to stitch them so they don't show.
4. Block (page 34) the finished pillow front so it measures 18″ × 18″.
5. Use the faux button back method (page 40), or any other pillow back, to finish the pillow.

The Perry
Zebra Stripe Intarsia Pillow

Finished size: 18″ × 18″

The pattern in this pillow uses intarsia knitting to place two fabric-yarns in a bold zebra stripe. In both combinations, 100% cotton quilting fabric is paired up with 100% polyester knit fleece. The traditional black-and-white variation matches a black knit with glow-in-the-dark fabric for the light portion of the stripe. In the other combination, a white knit is combined with citrusy tropical cotton.

What You'll Need

NEEDLES/GAUGE

Gauge (refer to page 32): 10 stitches per 4½″. Try size 9 needles, and adjust as needed.

FABRICS

Your yardage requirements may vary. Refer to Woven Fabric versus Knit Fabric (page 7) and Fabric-Yarn (page 14).

Fabric-Yarn

Fabric A: ½ yard 100% cotton quilting fabric, 44″–45″ wide, or the equivalent, for 51 yards of fabric-yarn

Fabric B: ⅝ yard 100% polyester waffle-knit fleece, 65″ wide, or the equivalent, for 51 yards of fabric-yarn

Pillow Back and Lining

Choose either the striped or solid zipper pillow back option (refer to page 42).

Option 1 – Striped Pillow Back: ¼ yard additional from each of fabrics A and B

Option 2 – Solid Pillow Back (Fabric C): ½ yard 100% cotton quilting fabric, 44″–45″ wide; use a coordinating fabric or an additional ½ yard of fabric A

Lining: ½ yard 100% cotton quilting fabric, 44″–45″ wide

NOTIONS

- Rotary cutter, ruler, and mat
- Decorative-edge rotary blade
- Fabric glue
- Large-eye yarn needle
- Medium crochet hook (optional)
- Sewing needle
- Sewing thread to match fabrics
- 1 zipper 16″ long to match backing fabric (optional)
- 20″ × 20″ batting (optional)
- 20″ × 20″ pillow form

Preparation

Refer to Ready, Set, Let's Start Strippin' (pages 13–23).

Fabric-Yarn A: Use a rotary cutter fit with a decorative-edge blade and a ruler to cut the fabric crosswise into ¼″ strips. Glue the ends together, and wind into 6 small balls of fabric-yarn.

Fabric-Yarn B: Use a rotary cutter and a ruler to cut the fabric crosswise into ½″ strips. Tie the ends together. Because the waffle knit will stretch, pull the fabric-yarn taut, and wind into 6 small balls of fabric-yarn.

 TIP from Mark *For some of the balls of yarn, join and wind only 2 fabric strips. This is just enough for small intarsia areas.*

Knitting

The EVEN rows, all purl stitches, are the wrong side of the pillow front. The ODD rows, all knit stitches, are the right side of the pillow front.

CAST ON

Fabric-Yarn A: Loosely cast on 47 stitches. This cast-on row is Row 1.

ROW 2

Follow the knitting chart on the next page. Start with Row 2, reading from *left* to *right*.

Purl all stitches, and tie on color changes crossing fabric-yarn (page 30) as indicated. This row has 10 color changes (5 for fabric-yarn A and 5 for fabric-yarn B).

ROW 3 AND ALL ODD ROWS

Follow the knitting chart, reading from *right* to *left*. Knit all stitches, crossing the fabric-yarn at the color changes.

Woven color joins of intarsia on back side of knit pillow

Fabrics for The Perry—Zebra Stripe Intarsia Pillow

ROW 4 AND ALL EVEN ROWS

Follow the knitting chart, reading from *left* to *right*. Purl all stitches, crossing the fabric-yarn at the color changes.

CONTINUE KNITTING

Continue following the knitting chart, working all ODD and EVEN rows as described. Tie on new fabric-yarn as needed. Work knots and joins on the wrong (purl) side of the work.

Finishing

Refer to pages 33–35.

1. Using fabric-yarn A, loosely bind off (page 33) all the stitches (Row 80).
2. Use the large-eye needle or crochet hook to weave the loose tail ends of the fabric-yarn into the body of the work or along the finished edges.
3. If necessary, hide the ends of the fabric-yarn by using a sewing needle and thread to stitch them so they don't show.
4. Block (page 34) the finished pillow front so it measures 18″ × 18″.
5. Use the zipper back method (pages 42–43), or any other pillow back, to finish the pillow.

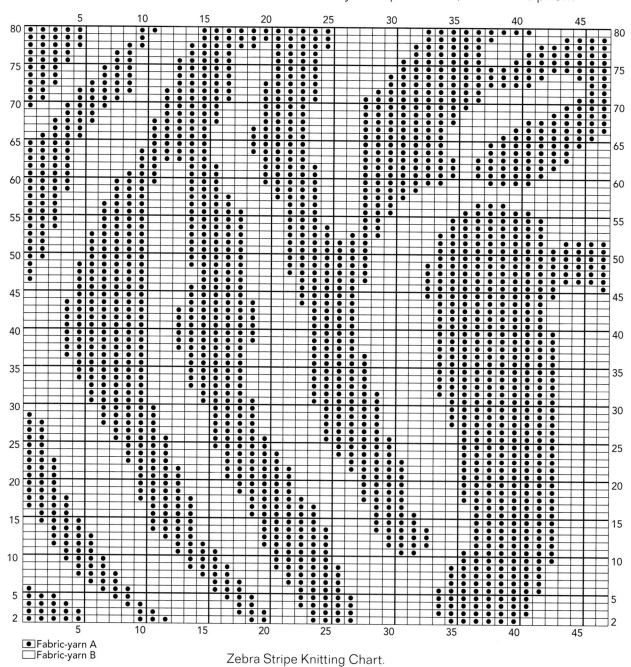

Fabric-yarn A
Fabric-yarn B

Zebra Stripe Knitting Chart.

Brushed Wool Throw
with Alternating Cables and Bi-Colored Stripes

Finished size: 38″ × 38″

Lofty fabric-yarn makes the chunky, alternately cabled throw lighter than it appears, and brushed or fleeced fabrics give this fun project a warm, fluffy attitude. The bi-colored stripes, one made of faux fur, add to the plush-toy feeling of the project. Wrap yourself up in the coziness!

Fabrics for Brushed Wool Throw with Alternating Cables and Bi-Colored Stripes

What You'll Need

NEEDLES/GAUGE

Gauge (refer to page 32): 4 stitches per 2″. Try size 17 needles, and adjust as needed.

FABRICS

Your yardage requirements may vary. Refer to Woven Fabric versus Knit Fabric (page 7) and Fabric-Yarn (page 14).

Fabric A: 3 yards spongy, lofty fabric such as brushed wool, polar fleece, or similar plush fabric, 60″ wide, or the equivalent, for 580–600 yards of fabric-yarn

Fabric B: ½ yard polyester faux fur, at least 44″–45″ wide, or the equivalent, for 20 yards of fabric-yarn

Fabric C: ¼ yard coordinating fabric, at least 44″–45″ wide, or the equivalent, for 12 yards of fabric-yarn

TIP from Mark

I am very pleased with the design of this throw, but the next time I knit one, I will knit it with bold stripes or make it scrappier by continuously tying on various compatible fabric-yarns as I knit. Your options are limited only by your imagination!

NOTIONS

- Rotary cutter, ruler, and mat
- Craft knife
- Coordinating or contrasting thread (I used 3 spools, each 500 yards)
- Large cable needle
- Large-eye yarn needle
- Medium crochet hook (optional)
- Sewing needle
- Sewing thread to match fabrics

Preparation

Refer to Ready, Set, Let's Start Strippin' (pages 13–23).

Fabric-Yarn A: Use a rotary cutter and a ruler to cut the fabric crosswise into ¼" strips. Sew the fabric strips together with a continuous zigzag stitch. You can wind the fabric-yarn into 1 huge ball (just for fun) or make several smaller, more manageable balls.

Fabric-Yarn B: From the wrong side, use a craft knife to cut the fabric *lengthwise* into a continuous ¼" strip (refer to page 17). Wind into 1 ball of fabric-yarn.

Fabric-Yarn C: Use a rotary cutter and a ruler to cut the fabric crosswise into ¼" strips. Tie the ends together, and wind into 1 ball of fabric-yarn.

Knitting

The cable is worked over 6 stitches (page 31) with repeats every 10 rows. The cable columns alternately cross as the rows are worked. ODD rows are the right side of the work and EVEN rows are the wrong side.

CAST ON

Fabric-Yarn A: Loosely cast on 76 stitches.

ROW 1

Knit 1 stitch. *Purl 2 stitches, Knit 6 stitches*. Repeat * to * 8 more times. Purl 2 stitches, and Knit 1 stitch.

ROW 2

Purl 1 stitch. *Knit 2 stitches, and Purl 6 stitches*. Repeat * to * 8 more times. Knit 2 stitches, and Purl 1 stitch.

ROW 3 – CABLE ROW

Knit 1 stitch, Purl 2 stitches, Knit 6 stitches, and Purl 2 stitches. Work the cable over the next 6 stitches: *Place the next 3 stitches on the cable needle to the back of the work. Knit 3 stitches off the knitting needle. Knit the 3 stitches off the cable needle.* *Purl 2 stitches, Knit 6 stitches, and Purl 2 stitches. Work the cable over the next 6 stitches*. Repeat * to * 2 more times. Purl 2 stitches, Knit 6 stitches, Purl 2 stitches, and Knit 1 stitch.

Make fast work of your knitting: on all rows except the cable and alternating cable rows, work the stitches as they appear on the needle. Purl the purl stitches, and Knit the knit stitches.

ROW 4 – COLOR STRIPE ROW

Tie on fabric-yarn B. Repeat Row 2.

ROWS 5 AND 7

Tie on fabric-yarn A. Repeat Row 1.

ROWS 6 AND 8

Repeat Row 2.

ROW 9 – ALTERNATING CABLE ROW

Knit 1 stitch. *Purl 2 stitches. Work the cable over the next 6 stitches (refer to Row 3). Purl 2 stitches, and Knit 6 stitches*. Repeat * to * 3 more times. Purl 2 stitches. Work the cable over the next 6 stitches. Purl 2 stitches, and Knit 1 stitch.

ROW 10

Repeat Row 2.

Now that you've mastered Rows 1–10, here's a quick tip for more advanced knitters: You'll work the remaining pattern in repeats of Rows 1–10, ending with Row 126. Fabric-yarn stripes (Color Stripe Rows) occur in Rows 34, 64, 94, and 124.

ROWS 11–30

Using fabric-yarn A, repeat Rows 1–10 two more times, without changing fabric-yarn on the Color Stripe Row.

ROWS 31–33

Using fabric-yarn A, repeat Rows 1–3.

ROW 34

Using fabric-yarn C, repeat Row 4 – Color Stripe Row.

ROWS 35–40

Using fabric-yarn A, repeat Rows 5–10.

ROWS 41–60

Using fabric-yarn A, repeat Rows 1–10 two more times, without changing fabric-yarn on the Color Stripe Row.

ROWS 61–63

Using fabric-yarn A, repeat Rows 1–3.

ROW 64

Using fabric-yarn B, repeat Row 4 – Color Stripe Row.

ROWS 65–70

Using fabric-yarn A, repeat Rows 5–10.

ROWS 71–90

Using fabric-yarn A, repeat Rows 1–10 two more times, without changing fabric-yarn on the Color Stripe Row.

ROWS 91–93

Using fabric-yarn A, repeat Rows 1–3.

ROW 94

Using fabric-yarn C, repeat Row 4 – Color Stripe Row.

ROWS 95–100

Using fabric-yarn A, repeat Rows 5–10.

ROWS 101–120

Using fabric-yarn A, repeat Rows 1–10 two more times, without changing fabric-yarn on the Color Stripe Row.

ROWS 121–123

Using fabric-yarn A, repeat Rows 1–3.

ROW 124

Using fabric-yarn B, repeat Row 4 – Color Stripe Row.

ROWS 125–126

Using fabric-yarn A, repeat Rows 5–6.

Finishing

Refer to pages 33–35.

1. Loosely bind off (page 33) all the stitches.
2. Use the large-eye needle or crochet hook to weave the loose tail ends of the fabric-yarn into the body of the work or along the finished edges.
3. If necessary, hide the ends of the fabric-yarn by using a sewing needle and thread to stitch them so they don't show.
4. Block (page 34) the finished throw (optional).

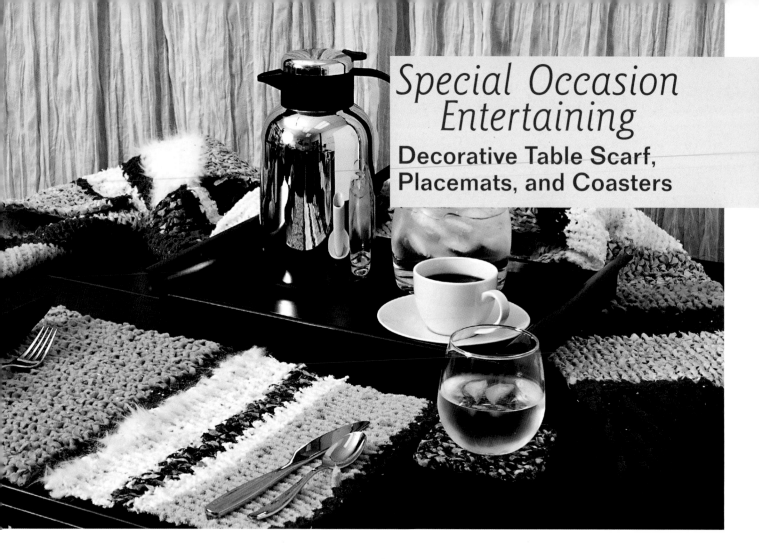

The knit table scarf is simply an enlarged scarf, and the placemats and coasters are scaled-down versions. Depending upon the fabrics used to create the fabric-yarn, these pieces are equally suited for holiday themes as well as bridal and baby showers, bar and bat mitzvahs, first communions, and wedding table settings. Be creative, as there are many ways to use this piece: wrap it on a banister entwined with tiny holiday lights, weave it through pine cones and branches on a mantel, or use it to add color and texture anywhere in the house.

Don't be surprised at the different fabrics used, including flannel, terry, and waffle knit—they knit up beautifully and provide fabulous color and surface appeal.

What You'll Need

NEEDLES/GAUGE

Gauge (refer to page 32): 5 stitches per 2″. Try size 11 needles. The gauge is not critical to the outcome of the projects, and different fabric-yarns will produce slightly different gauges.

FABRICS

Your yardage requirements may vary. Refer to Woven Fabric versus Knit Fabric (page 7) and Fabric-Yarn (page 14).

The following fabric requirements use the holiday fabrics indicated on the color chart on page 62.

Fabric A: 1¾ yards 100% cotton flannel, 44″–45″ wide, or the equivalent, for 260 yards of fabric-yarn

Fabric B: 1¼ yards 100% cotton waffle knit, 65″ wide, or the equivalent, for 275 yards of fabric-yarn (Note: Because waffle knit will double in length when made into fabric-yarn, less fabric is required.)

Fabric C: ¼ yard cotton-blend terry cloth, 60″ wide, or the equivalent, for 45–50 yards of fabric-yarn (Note: Because terry cloth will double in length when made into fabric-yarn, less fabric is required.)

Fabric D: ¾ yard 100% cotton quilting fabric, 44″–45″ wide, or the equivalent, for 85–90 yards of fabric-yarn

Fabric E: ¼ yard 100% cotton quilting fabric, 44″–45″ wide, or the equivalent, for 22–25 yards of fabric-yarn

Fabric F: ¾ yard wool/cashmere blend, 56″ wide, or the equivalent, for 110 yards of fabric-yarn

Fabric G: ½ yard 100% cotton quilting fabric, 44″–45″ wide, or the equivalent, for 45–50 yards of fabric-yarn

Fabric H: ½ yard faux fur, at least 44″–45″ wide, or the equivalent, for 45–50 yards of fabric-yarn

Fabric I: ½ yard 100% cotton quilting fabric, 44″–45″ wide, or the equivalent, for 45–50 yards of fabric yarn

> **TIP from Mark**
>
> *Be ready for any special occasion. Follow the color chart provided for a holiday theme, or choose a different combination to change the theme of your scarf, placemats, and coasters. You need approximately 950 yards of fabric-yarn if you want to create your own color combinations.*

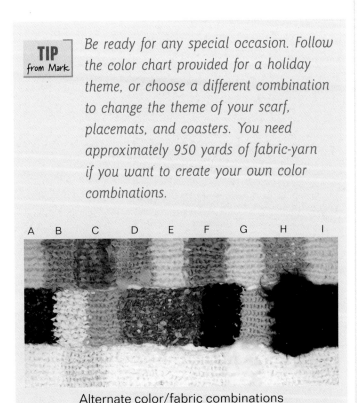

A B C D E F G H I

Alternate color/fabric combinations

NOTIONS

- Rotary cutter, ruler, and mat
- Decorative-edge rotary blade
- Fabric glue
- Craft knife
- Large-eye yarn needle
- Medium crochet hook (optional)
- Sewing needle
- Sewing thread to match fabrics

Fabric options for Special Occasion Entertaining

Preparation

Refer to Ready, Set, Let's Start Strippin' (pages 13–23).

Fabric-Yarn A: Use a rotary cutter fit with a decorative-edge blade to cut the fabric *lengthwise* into ¼″ strips. Overlap ends, and machine backtack to join the fabric strips. Wind into 1 ball of fabric-yarn.

Fabric-Yarn B: Use a rotary cutter and a ruler to cut the fabric crosswise into ½″ strips. Tie the ends of the fabric strips together. Because waffle knit stretches, pull the fabric-yarn taut, and wind into 1 ball of fabric-yarn.

Fabric-Yarn C: Use a rotary cutter and a ruler to cut the fabric crosswise into ¼″ strips. Tie the ends of the fabric strips together. Because terry cloth stretches, pull the fabric-yarn taut, and wind into 1 ball of fabric-yarn.

Fabric-Yarn D: Use a rotary cutter and a ruler to cut the fabric crosswise into ¼″ strips. Glue the fabric strips together, and make 2 equal balls of fabric-yarn. You'll knit 2 of fabric-yarn D at the same time.

Fabric-Yarn E: Use a rotary cutter fit with a decorative-edge blade to cut the fabric crosswise into ¼″ strips. Tie the fabric strips together, and wind into 1 ball of fabric-yarn.

Fabric-Yarn F: Use a rotary cutter fit with a decorative-edge blade to cut the fabric crosswise into ¼″ strips. Overlap the ends, and backtack to join the fabric strips together. Wind into 1 ball of fabric-yarn.

Fabric-Yarn G: Use a rotary cutter fit with a decorative-edge blade to cut the fabric crosswise into ¼″ strips. Overlap the ends, and machine bar tack to join the fabric strips together. Wind into 1 ball of fabric-yarn.

Fabric-Yarn H: From the wrong side of the fabric, use a craft knife to cut the fabric *lengthwise* into a continuous ¼″ strip of fabric-yarn (refer to page 17). Wind into 1 ball of fabric-yarn.

Fabric-Yarn I: Use a rotary cutter and a ruler to cut the fabric crosswise into ¼″ strips. Glue the fabric strips together, and wind into 1 ball of fabric-yarn.

Holiday Table Scarf

Finished size: 11″ × 96″

Knitting

The table scarf is worked with a 1 × 1 rib (page 28) over an ODD number of stitches for many rows of color change.

CAST ON

Fabric-Yarn A: Loosely cast on 27 stitches.

ALL ROWS

Work all rows in a 1 × 1 rib.

CONTINUE KNITTING

Refer to the chart at right for the number of rows to knit for each color change. Working in the 1 × 1 rib stitch, tie on a new fabric-yarn (page 29) for each color change. Knit all 363 rows, or until you achieve the desired length.

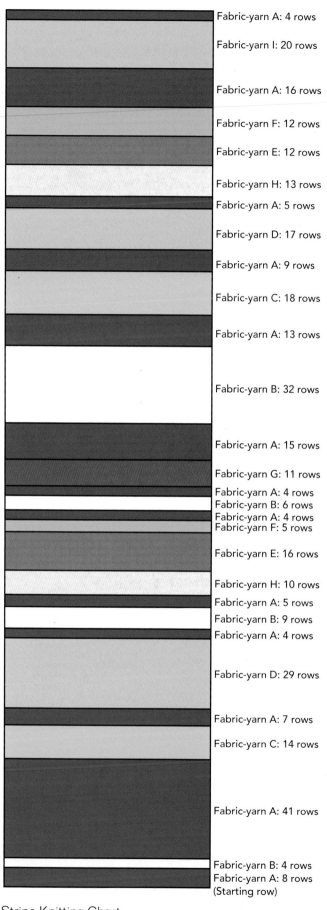

Fabric-yarn A: 4 rows

Fabric-yarn I: 20 rows

Fabric-yarn A: 16 rows

Fabric-yarn F: 12 rows

Fabric-yarn E: 12 rows

Fabric-yarn H: 13 rows

Fabric-yarn A: 5 rows

Fabric-yarn D: 17 rows

Fabric-yarn A: 9 rows

Fabric-yarn C: 18 rows

Fabric-yarn A: 13 rows

Fabric-yarn B: 32 rows

Fabric-yarn A: 15 rows

Fabric-yarn G: 11 rows

Fabric-yarn A: 4 rows
Fabric-yarn B: 6 rows
Fabric-yarn A: 4 rows
Fabric-yarn F: 5 rows

Fabric-yarn E: 16 rows

Fabric-yarn H: 10 rows

Fabric-yarn A: 5 rows

Fabric-yarn B: 9 rows

Fabric-yarn A: 4 rows

Fabric-yarn D: 29 rows

Fabric-yarn A: 7 rows

Fabric-yarn C: 14 rows

Fabric-yarn A: 41 rows

Fabric-yarn B: 4 rows
Fabric-yarn A: 8 rows
(Starting row)

Stripe Knitting Chart

Finishing

Refer to pages 33–35.

1. Loosely bind off (page 33) all the stitches.
2. Use the large-eye needle or crochet hook to weave the loose tail ends of the fabric-yarn into the body of the work or along the finished edges.
3. If necessary, hide the ends of the fabric-yarn by using a sewing needle and thread to stitch them so they don't show.
4. Block (page 34) the finished scarf.
5. Use fabric-yarn A to add a fringe (page 35).

Striped Placemats

Finished size: 14″ × 19″

Use fabric-yarn leftovers from the Holiday Table Scarf to create a matching set of placemats. Or use leftovers from any other project in this book for everyday-use placemats. Cotton is perfect and can be machine washed, with only 5% shrinkage.

Knitting

Refer to the Stripe Knitting Chart on the previous page and select a section of stripes to use working in a 1 × 1 rib, or follow your own muse, changing colors as the mood strikes.

CAST ON

Cast on 35 stitches.

ALL ROWS

Work all rows in a 1 × 1 rib over an ODD number of stitches (refer to page 28).

CONTINUE KNITTING

Continue the 1 × 1 rib, tying on and changing colors as desired. Because the gauge will vary with your fabric choices (refer to page 32), knit until the placemat measures 19″.

 TIP from Mark *As a general rule of thumb, knit fabrics will produce more fabric-yarn, whereas lofty, bulky fabrics will produce far less.*

Finishing

Refer to pages 33–35.

1. Loosely bind off (page 33) all the stitches.
2. Use the large-eye needle or crochet hook to weave the loose tail ends of the fabric-yarn into the body of the work or along the finished edges.
3. If necessary, hide the ends of the fabric-yarn by using a sewing needle and thread to stitch them so they don't show.
4. Block (page 34) each placemat so it measures 14″ × 19″.

Coasters

Finished size: 4″ × 4″

Select fabrics and prepare the fabric-yarn according to the instructions above for the table scarf (pages 60–62). You can make the coasters from the same fabric-yarn or leftover fabrics, or choose 8 different fabrics. You need 25 yards of fabric-yarn for each coaster; ⅜ yard of 100% cotton quilting fabric, 44″-45″ wide, yields approximately 50 yards of ¼″-wide fabric-yarn.

Knitting

Work the coasters using a 1 × 1 rib (page 28).

CAST ON

Cast on 12 stitches.

ALL ROWS

Work in a 1 × 1 rib over an ODD number of stitches.
Knit until the piece is square (refer to the tip on page 48).

Finishing

Refer to pages 33–35.

1. Bind off (page 33) all the stitches.
2. Use the large-eye needle or crochet hook to weave the loose tail ends of the fabric-yarn into the body of the work or along the finished edges.
3. If necessary, hide the ends of the fabric-yarn by using a sewing needle and thread to stitch them so they don't show.
4. Block (page 34) each finished coaster so it measures 4″ × 4″.

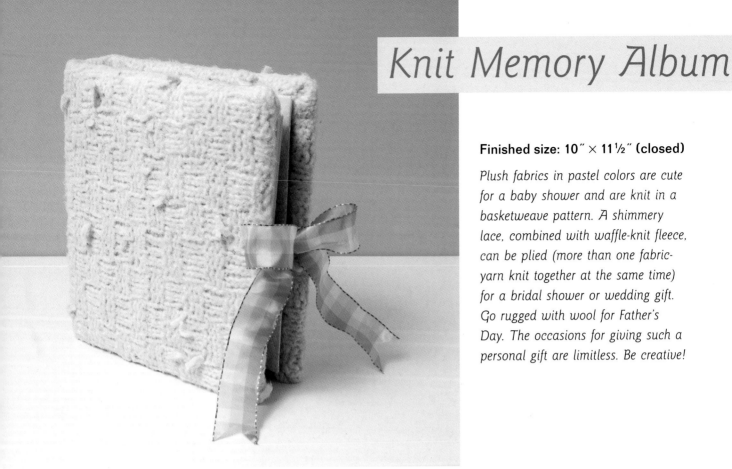

Knit Memory Album

Finished size: 10″ × 11½″ (closed)

Plush fabrics in pastel colors are cute for a baby shower and are knit in a basketweave pattern. A shimmery lace, combined with waffle-knit fleece, can be plied (more than one fabric-yarn knit together at the same time) for a bridal shower or wedding gift. Go rugged with wool for Father's Day. The occasions for giving such a personal gift are limitless. Be creative!

What You'll Need

NEEDLES/GAUGE

Gauge (refer to page 32): 7 stitches per 2½″ worked in basketweave stitch. Try size 9 needles, and adjust as needed.

FABRICS

Your yardage requirements may vary. Refer to Woven Fabric versus Knit Fabric (page 7) and Fabric-Yarn (page 14).

Fabric: ½ yard polar fleece or other plush knit fabric, 60″ wide, or the equivalent, for 85 yards of fabric-yarn

Lining: 1 yard 100% cotton quilting fabric, 44″–45″ wide

Fabrics for Knit Memory Album

NOTIONS

- Rotary cutter, ruler, and mat
- Large-eye yarn needle
- Medium crochet hook (optional)
- Sewing needle
- Sewing thread to match fabrics
- 1 purchased photo album, 10″ × 11½″
- Craft glue
- Wooden craft sticks
- Medium-weight cardboard
- 13″ × 24″ batting, ¾″ thickness or less
- Pins
- 1 yard wire-edge ribbon, 1¼″ wide, to match knit album cover

Preparation

Refer to Ready, Set, Let's Start Strippin' (pages 13–23).

Fabric-Yarn: Use a rotary cutter and a ruler to cut the fabric crosswise into ¼″ strips. Tie the ends of the fabric strips together, and wind into 1 ball of fabric-yarn.

Knitting

The Memory Album is knit in the basketweave stitch. The textured pattern is knit lengthwise to cover the album, giving the project a fresh and unique look.

CAST ON

Fabric-Yarn: Loosely cast on 35 stitches.

ROWS 1–8

Work rows 1–8 in basketweave stitch, following the directions on page 29.

CONTINUE KNITTING

Repeat Rows 1–8 until the piece measures 24".

Finishing

Refer to pages 33–35.

1. Loosely bind off (page 33) all the stitches.
2. Use the large-eye needle or crochet hook to weave the loose tail ends of the fabric-yarn into the body of the work or along the finished edges.
3. If necessary, hide the ends of the fabric-yarn by using a sewing needle and thread to stitch them so they don't show.
4. Block (page 34) the piece to measure 13" × 24".

Assembling the Memory Album

INSIDE COVER PREPARATION

1. From the lining fabric, cut 2 pieces 3" × 11" for the spine.
2. Use a wooden stick to spread craft glue along the metal spine on the inside front cover of the photo album. Slide a long edge of one 3" × 11" lining piece under the metal spine of the inside cover, centering it top to bottom. Trim any extra fabric even with the sides of the album. Repeat for the back cover.

Cover the inside spine with the lining fabric.

3. Measure *both* inside front and back covers of the photo album and subtract ½". Cut 2 pieces of cardboard to fit these measurements. With a pencil, label the cardboard as front or back.

 TIP from Mark *Be aware that some albums do not fold evenly at the spine; the inside back cover might be a larger size than the inside front cover, or vice versa. This is why it is important to measure both inside covers.*

4. From the lining fabric, cut 2 pieces 1½" larger than the cut cardboard front and back cover pieces.
5. Place the just-cut fabric lining pieces wrong side up on the work surface. Center the corresponding cut cardboard pieces, label side up, on top of the fabric.

Center the cardboard on the lining fabric.

6. Prepare one pairing of fabric and cardboard at a time. With a wooden craft stick, spread a small amount of craft glue on each of the 4 corners. Bring up the corners of the fabric and secure them in place. Repeat for the other pairing.

7. Spread glue along the straight sides of the cardboard. Fold the fabric over, and secure it to the glue. Repeat for all 4 sides of both linings.

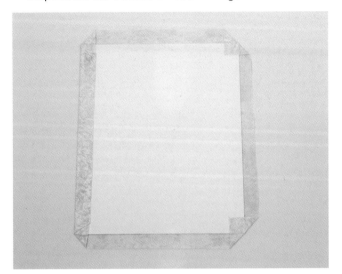

Center and glue the cardboard pieces to the lining.

OUTSIDE COVER

1. From the lining fabric, cut 1 piece 13″ × 24″ for the album cover.

2. Place the batting flat on the work surface. Center the open photo album, cover side down, on the batting. Trace around all 4 sides of the album, and remove it gently, so as not to disturb the batting. Cut out the batting along the tracing lines.

3. Place the 13″ × 24″ lining fabric flat on the work surface, wrong side up. Center the cut piece of batting on the lining fabric. Align the open photo album, cover side down, on the batting. Make sure the front of the photo album is to your left and that the batting does not extend too far past the edges of the covers.

Lining, batting, and photo album

4. With a wooden craft stick, spread a small amount of craft glue on each of the 4 corners, as you did with the cardboard and lining. Bring up the corners of the fabric and secure them in place on the inside covers.

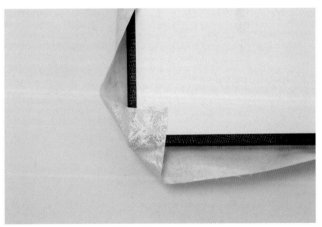

Glue and fold the fabric over the edges.

5. Start near the spine of the photo album and the 3″ × 11″ lining piece. Spread the glue along the bottom edge of the inside front cover. Fold the fabric over, and secure it to the glue. Repeat for the top edges.

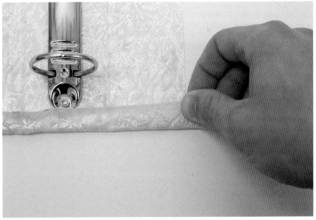

Glue the sides.

6. In the same manner as in Step 5, spread glue and fold the fabric over the straight side edges of the inside front and back covers.

7. Allow the album to dry for several hours.

8. Place the fabric-yarn album cover flat on the work surface, with the cast-on edge to your left.

9. Center the open photo album, cover side down, on the knit cover. Make sure the front of the photo album is to your left. Repeat Steps 4–7 with the knit cover.

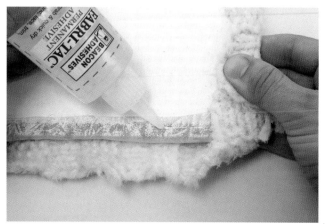

Glue and fold the knit cover over the edges.

10. Cut the wire-edge ribbon in half. Glue a 2″ tab of ribbon to each of the inside covers, centering the ribbon top to bottom. The ribbon is used to tie the album closed.

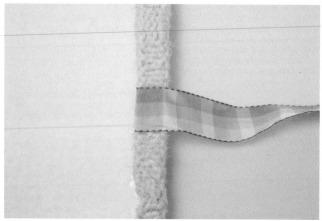

Glue the ribbon.

11. Apply glue to the wrong side of the lined cardboard pieces. Align the glued cardboard pieces to the appropriate inside covers, concealing the glued edges of the fabric- and knit-covered photo album.

12. Weight the glued cardboard lining with books or other heavy objects for several hours until the glue dries.

Finished size: 8″ × 8″

The Pacifier Pillow is knit from a plush fabric-yarn and embellished with pacifiers, rattles, and diaper pins—a perfect baby shower gift. The Ring Bearer Pillow uses lace and a polyester fleece fabric-yarn, knit as one, to create an elegant but soft-textured pillow top. Gold rings make the pillow ready for that special day. I guarantee you'll find yourself making these again and again.

Ring Bearer or Pacifier Pillow

What You'll Need

NEEDLES/GAUGE

Gauge (refer to page 32): 4 stitches per 2″. Try size 11 needles, and adjust as needed.

FABRICS

Your yardage requirements may vary. Refer to Woven Fabric versus Knit Fabric (page 7) and Fabric-Yarn (page 14).

Note: Use the yardage for either the Pacifier Pillow **OR** the Ring Bearer Pillow.

Pacifier Pillow

Fabric A: ½ yard 100% cotton or polyester fleece knit fabric, 60″ wide, or the equivalent, for 85 yards of fabric-yarn

Pillow Lining: ⅜ yard 100% cotton quilting fabric, 44–45″ wide, or 3 squares 9″ × 9″

Ring Bearer Pillow

Fabric B: ¾ yard lace, 45″ wide, or the equivalent, for 85 yards of fabric-yarn (I have found that lace that has a 3-dimensional texture holds together much better than flat-surfaced lace.) Note: The lace will stretch, so less fabric is required.

Fabric C: ½ yard 100% cotton or polyester fleece knit fabric, 60″ wide, or the equivalent, for 85 yards of fabric-yarn

Pillow Lining: ⅜ yard 100% cotton quilting fabric, 44″–45″ wide, or 3 squares 9″ × 9″

Fabrics for Ring Bearer Pillow

NOTIONS

- Rotary cutter, ruler, and mat
- Rhinestone setter (optional)
- Medium crochet hook (optional)
- Large-eye yarn needle
- Sewing needle
- Sewing thread to match fabrics
- 8″ × 8″ batting
- Polyester fiberfill
- 1 yard each of ⅛″-wide satin and sheer ribbons
- Embellishments: pacifiers, rings, ribbons, beads, feathers, pearls, or other small items

Preparation

Refer to Ready, Set, Let's Start Strippin' (pages 13–23).

Pacifier Pillow

Fabric-Yarn A: Use a rotary cutter and a ruler to cut the fabric crosswise into ¼″ strips. Tie the ends together, and wind into 1 ball of fabric-yarn.

Ring Bearer Pillow

Fabric-Yarn B: Use a rotary cutter and a ruler to cut the fabric crosswise into ½″ strips. Join the overlapped ends of the fabric strips together with a rhinestone setter. Because the lace will stretch, pull the fabric-yarn taut, and wind into 1 ball of fabric-yarn.

Fabric-Yarn C: Use a rotary cutter and a ruler to cut the fabric crosswise into ¼″ strips. Tie the ends together, and wind into 1 ball of fabric-yarn.

Knitting

For the Pacifier Pillow, work 1 strand of fabric-yarn A. For the Ring Bearer Pillow, work, or ply, fabric-yarns B and C together as 1 fabric-yarn. Knit the small pillow top in stockinette stitch (page 27).

CAST ON

Loosely cast on 16 stitches.

ROW 1 AND ALL ODD ROWS

Knit all stitches.

ROW 2 AND ALL EVEN ROWS

Purl all stitches.

CONTINUE KNITTING

Repeat Rows 1 and 2 until the piece measures 8″ square (refer to the tip on page 48).

Finishing

Refer to pages 33–35.

1. Loosely bind off (page 33) all the stitches.
2. Use the large-eye needle or crochet hook to weave the loose tail ends of the fabric-yarn into the body of the work or along the finished edges.
3. If necessary, hide the ends of the fabric-yarn by using a sewing needle and thread to stitch them so they don't show.
4. Block (page 34) the piece to measure 8″ × 8″.

Making the Pillow

1. From the lining fabric, cut 3 squares 9″ × 9″.
2. Center the 8″ × 8″ square of batting on the wrong side of one of the 9″ × 9″ squares of lining fabric.

Center the batting on the lining.

3. Place another 9″ × 9″ square of lining fabric right side up on top of the batting. Pin around all 4 sides to secure the pieces together. Quilt or stitch as desired.

Layered backing

4. Turn under, toward the wrong side, a ½″ seam allowance along all 4 sides of the layered and quilted square. Baste the seam allowance. Repeat for the remaining 9″ × 9″ lining square.

5. Align the lining square with the quilted square, wrong sides together. Pin and baste the layers together around 3 sides. On a sewing machine, edgestitch around the 3 basted sides.

Pieces layered and ready for machine edgestitching

6. Stuff the little fabric pillowcase with fiberfill. Baste the last (open) side together and machine edgestitch it closed.

7. Hand stitch the knit pillow top to the unquilted side of the pillow with a needle and matching thread.

8. Embellish with ribbons, feathers, and beads as desired. Tie pacifiers, rattles, or rings to the knit pillow top.

Fashion

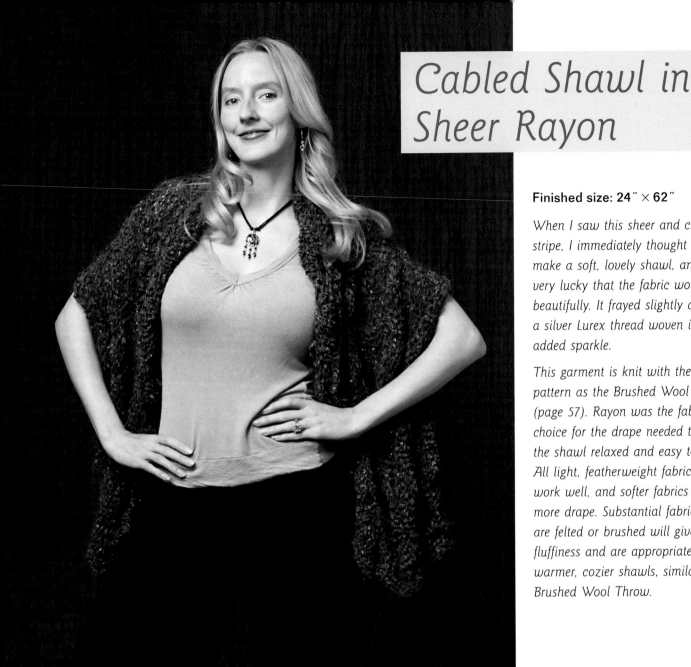

Cabled Shawl in Sheer Rayon

Finished size: 24″ × 62″

When I saw this sheer and chenille stripe, I immediately thought it would make a soft, lovely shawl, and I was very lucky that the fabric worked beautifully. It frayed slightly and had a silver Lurex thread woven in for added sparkle.

This garment is knit with the same pattern as the Brushed Wool Throw (page 57). Rayon was the fabric of choice for the drape needed to make the shawl relaxed and easy to wear. All light, featherweight fabrics will work well, and softer fabrics will give more drape. Substantial fabrics that are felted or brushed will give a lofty fluffiness and are appropriate for warmer, cozier shawls, similar to the Brushed Wool Throw.

What You'll Need

NEEDLES/GAUGE

Gauge (refer to page 32): 4 stitches per 2″. Try size 11 needles, and adjust as needed.

FABRICS

Your yardage requirements may vary. Refer to Woven Fabric versus Knit Fabric (page 7) and Fabric-Yarn (page 14).

Fabric: 1¾ yards 100% rayon, 53″–54″ wide, or the equivalent, for 312 yards of fabric-yarn

Fabric for Cabled Shawl in Sheer Rayon

NOTIONS

- Rotary cutter, ruler, and mat
- Fabric glue
- Large cable needle
- Large-eye yarn needle
- Medium crochet hook (optional)
- Sewing needle
- Sewing thread to match fabric

Preparation

Refer to Ready, Set, Let's Start Strippin' (pages 13–23).

Fabric-Yarn: Use a rotary cutter and a ruler to cut the fabric crosswise into ¼″ strips. Glue the fabric strips together, and wind into 1 ball of fabric-yarn.

 Precut rayon strips are available on the market to make this a quick project (refer to Resources on page 94).

Knitting

The cable is worked over 6 stitches and 10 rows. The cable columns alternately cross as the rows are worked. ODD rows are the right side of the work and EVEN rows are the wrong side.

CAST ON

Fabric-Yarn: Loosely cast on 124 stitches.

ROW 1

Knit 1 stitch. *Purl 2 stitches, and Knit 6 stitches*. Repeat * to * 14 more times. Purl 2 stitches, and Knit 1 stitch.

ROW 2

Purl 1 stitch. *Knit 2 stitches, and Purl 6 stitches*. Repeat * to * 14 more times. Knit 2 stitches, and Purl 1 stitch.

ROW 3 – CABLE ROW

Knit 1 stitch, Purl 2 stitches, Knit 6 stitches, and Purl 2 stitches. Work the cable over the next 6 stitches (refer to page 31): *Place the next 3 stitches on the cable needle to the back of the work. Knit 3 stitches off the knitting needle. Knit the 3 stitches off the cable needle.* *Purl 2 stitches, Knit 6 stitches, and Purl 2 stitches. Work the cable over the next 6 stitches*. Repeat * to * 5 more times. Purl 2 stitches, Knit 6 stitches, Purl 2 stitches, and Knit 1 stitch.

ROWS 4, 6, AND 8

Repeat Row 2.

ROWS 5 AND 7

Repeat Row 1.

ROW 9 – ALTERNATING CABLE ROW

Knit 1 stitch. *Purl 2 stitches. Work the cable over the next 6 stitches (refer to Row 3). Purl 2 stitches, and Knit 6 stitches*. Repeat * to * 6 more times. Purl 2 stitches. Work the cable over the next 6 stitches. Purl 2 stitches, and Knit 1 stitch.

ROW 10

Repeat Row 2.

CONTINUE KNITTING

Repeat Rows 1–10 until the piece measures 24″.

Finishing

Refer to pages 33–35.

1. Loosely bind off (page 33) all the stitches.
2. Use the large-eye needle or crochet hook to weave the loose tail ends of the fabric-yarn into the body of the work or along the finished edges.
3. If necessary, hide the ends of the fabric-yarn by using a sewing needle and thread to stitch them so they don't show.
4. Block (page 34) the finished shawl.

Lengthwise-Knit Garter Stitch Scarf

in a Cashmere/Wool Blend

Finished size: 9″ × 70″

This scarf is very fun to make and reminds me of a Slinky since it is knit lengthwise with a simple garter stitch. The ombré color effect is created with the fabric-yarn by sewing three colors together in a repeated order.

What You'll Need

NEEDLES/GAUGE

Gauge (refer to page 32): 3½ stitches per 2″. Try size 17 needles, and adjust as needed.

FABRICS

Your yardage requirements may vary. Refer to Woven Fabric versus Knit Fabric (page 7) and Fabric-Yarn (page 14).

Fabric A: ⅜ yard wool-blend fabric such as cashmere/wool, 100% wool, or wool/nylon, 56″ wide
Fabric B: ⅜ yard wool-blend fabric such as cashmere/wool, 100% wool, or wool/nylon, 56″ wide

Fabric C: ⅜ yard wool-blend fabric such as cashmere/wool, 100% wool, or wool/nylon, 56″ wide
The entire scarf requires the equivalent of 90–100 yards of fabric-yarn. If any other combination of fabric is used, yardages should be adjusted accordingly.

NOTIONS

- Rotary cutter, ruler, and mat
- Decorative-edge rotary blade
- Large-eye yarn needle
- Medium crochet hook (optional)
- Sewing needle
- Sewing thread to match fabrics

Fabrics for Lengthwise-Knit Garter Stitch Scarf

Preparation

Refer to Ready, Set, Let's Start Strippin' (pages 13–23).

Fabrics A, B, and C: For each fabric, use a rotary cutter fit with a decorative-edge blade to cut the fabric crosswise into ¼″ strips. Keep the fabrics separated by color. Make the fabric-yarn by joining 1 strip of each fabric-yarn in order: A to B to C. Join the strips by sewing the overlapped ends together with a backtack. Wind into 1 ball of fabric-yarn.

Knitting

This simple scarf pattern uses a garter stitch (page 28). All the rows are knit.

CAST ON

Fabric-Yarn A-B-C: Loosely cast on 124 stitches.

ALL ROWS

Knit all 124 stitches.

CONTINUE KNITTING

Continue knitting until the scarf measures 9″ wide.

Finishing

Refer to pages 33–35.

1. Very loosely bind off (page 33) all the stitches.
2. Use the large-eye needle or crochet hook to weave the loose tail ends of the fabric-yarn into the body of the work or along the finished edges.
3. If necessary, hide the ends of the fabric-yarn by using a sewing needle and thread to stitch them so they don't show.
4. Block (page 34) the finished scarf.
5. Cut fringe from the remaining fabric-yarn A-B-C, and weave it through stitches on the short sides of the scarf (page 35).
6. Trim the beginning and ending yarn to match the fringe length.

Braided Illusion Scarf
Knit in One Piece

Finished size: 6″ × 55″

Technically this scarf is one piece, but it is knit in smaller, more manageable sections. As with many projects in this book, it appears more complicated to complete than it actually is. Made in the right fabric, as pictured here in a fine-gauge knit with embossed glitter, this will become the piece around which you can build a wardrobe.

A knit fabric is essential for this project, and T-shirt-weight jersey, or spandex with lots of surface appeal, will work well. The more surface shimmer, the better!

Fabric for Braided Illusion Scarf

What You'll Need

NEEDLES/GAUGE

Gauge (refer to page 32): 4 stitches per 1″. Try size 11 needles, and adjust as needed.

FABRIC

Your yardage requirements may vary. Refer to Woven Fabric versus Knit Fabric (page 7) and Fabric-Yarn (page 14).

Fabric: 1¼ yards fine-knit fabric, at least 36″ wide, or the equivalent, for 276 yards of fabric-yarn (Note: Because knits will double in length when made into fabric-yarn, less fabric is required.)

NOTIONS

- Rotary cutter, ruler, and mat
- Stitch markers (optional)
- 4 double-pointed knitting needles with point protectors in same size as project needles (optional)
- Stitch holders (optional)
- T-pins
- Foamcore board or similar for braiding scarf
- Large-eye yarn needle
- Medium crochet hook (optional)
- Sewing needle
- Sewing thread to match fabrics

Preparation

Refer to Ready, Set, Let's Start Strippin' (pages 13–23).

Fabric-Yarn: Use a rotary cutter and a ruler to cut the fabric crosswise into ¼" strips. Tie the strips together. Because knits will stretch, pull the fabric-yarn taut as you wind it into 3 balls of the same size.

Knitting

This scarf is worked in a 1 × 1 rib (page 28) over an ODD number of stitches. The 27 stitches are split into 3 sets of 9 stitches, and worked separately to form 3 strips, which are then braided together.

CAST ON

Fabric-Yarn: Cast on 27 stitches.

ROW 1

Knit 1 stitch, and Purl 1 stitch. Repeat * to * across the remaining stitches, ending with a knit stitch.

ROW 2

Purl 1 stitch, and Knit 1 stitch. Repeat * to * across the remaining stitches, ending with a purl stitch.

DIVIDE STITCHES

In Row 3, the 27 stitches will be divided into 3 sets of 9 stitches each, with each set worked independently from its own ball of fabric-yarn. You may work each set of stitches with one knitting needle, with the stitches divided by stitch markers, or you may work each set on its own double-pointed needle. To keep the stitches from falling off, use point protectors.

ROW 3

Knit 1 stitch, and Purl 1 stitch for 9 stitches. Place a stitch marker, or place these just-worked stitches on a double-pointed needle secured with point protectors. Tie on a new ball of fabric-yarn (page 29). Knit 1 stitch, and Purl 1 stitch across the next 9 stitches. Place a stitch marker, or place these just-worked stitches on a double-pointed needle secured with point protectors or a stitch holder. Tie on a new ball of fabric-yarn. Knit 1 stitch, and Purl 1 stitch across the 9 remaining stitches. If desired, place these just-worked stitches on a double-pointed needle secured with point protectors.

WORKING STRIP SETS

Work each set of 9 stitches independently, using its own ball of fabric-yarn, and working stitches in a 1 × 1 rib.

If you are working with one needle and stitches divided with stitch markers, work each row by knitting across all 27 stitches. Pick up the next fabric-yarn ball for each strip set when you reach the stitch marker.

If you are working with double-pointed needles, each strip can be worked independently from its own fabric-yarn ball.

ROW 4 AND ALL REMAINING EVEN ROWS

Purl 1 stitch, and Knit 1 stitch, across each set of 9 stitches.

ROW 5 AND ALL REMAINING ODD ROWS

Knit 1 stitch, and Purl 1 stitch, across each set of 9 stitches.

CONTINUE KNITTING

Repeat Rows 4 and 5 for each set of 9 stitches until each strip measures 50", ending with an EVEN row. Loosely bind off (page 33) each set of 9 stitches.

BRAID

1. Secure the cast-on stitches to a foamcore board with T-pins.
2. Braid the 3 strips together along their full length. Avoid twisting the strips.
3. Use T-pins to secure the bottom of the braid, right side up, to the foamcore board, to keep it from unwinding.

FRINGE

1. Cut 34 lengths, 6″ long, of fabric-yarn for the fringe.
2. Evenly align the bound-off edge of each set of 9 stitches on the foamcore board. The aligned sets of stitches number, from left to right, 1–9, 10–18, and 19–27.

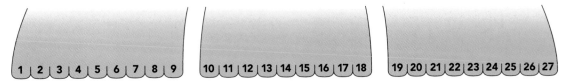

Numbered stitch sets.

3. Position the first knit strip (stitches 1–9) on top of the second strip (stitches 10–18), aligning the stitches as shown. Attach a piece of fringe (refer to page 35) to join stitches 5 and 10, 6 and 11, 7 and 12, and 8 and 13 together.

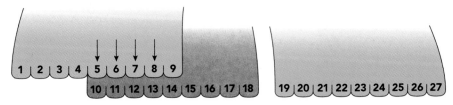

Align and attach the fringe.

4. Position the third knit strip (stitches 19–27) on top of the first and second strips, aligning the stitches as shown. Attach a piece of fringe to join stitches 19, 9, and 14; 20 and 15; 21 and 16; 22 and 17; and 23 and 18 together.

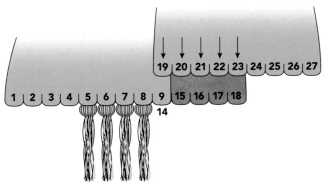

Align and attach the fringe.

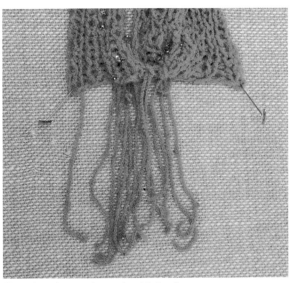

Overlap the ends and add the fringe.

5. Attach the fringe to the remaining stitches on the edge of the scarf—stitches 1–4 and 24–27.
6. Attach the remaining fringe to the cast-on edge of the scarf. Allow the strips to naturally overlap, and use fringe to secure the strips in place.
7. Trim all the fringe lengths even at the bottom.

Finishing

Refer to pages 33–35.

1. Use the large-eye needle and leftover fabric-yarn to sew and secure the 3 strips together at each braid crossing.
2. Use the large-eye needle or crochet hook to weave the loose tail ends of the fabric-yarn into the body of the work or along the finished edges.
3. If necessary, hide the ends of the fabric-yarn by using a sewing needle and thread to stitch them so they don't show.

The Tippi
Feathered and Felted-Wool Rib Knit Hat

Sizes: Adult Small to Extra Extra Large

The organic, natural textures and colors of the felted wool immediately reminded me of a bird's nest. Which, in turn, led me to think, naturally, of feathers, and feathers made me think of Hitchcock's movie The Birds. *Thus The Tippi was created. Initially developed more for the technique of incorporating feathers into the fabric-yarn as it was stitched, the more I experimented the more inspired I became.*

What You'll Need

NEEDLES/GAUGE

Gauge (refer to page 32): 2 stitches per 1″. Try size 10 needles, and adjust as needed.

FABRICS

Your yardage requirements may vary. Refer to Woven Fabric versus Knit Fabric (page 7) and Fabric-Yarn (page 14).

Soft, plush fabrics such as brushed or felted wool, polar fleece, and lofty cotton knits are the fabrics of choice for this project. They are warm and cozy and feel comfortable against the head when worn. I think you'll find yourself wearing this knit hat time and time again.

Fabric A: ¼ yard felted wool, 44″–45″ wide
Fabric B: 1 fat quarter felted wool (18″ × 22″)
Fabric C: 1 fat quarter felted wool (18″ × 22″)
Fabric D: 1 fat quarter felted wool (18″ × 22″)
Fabric E: 1 fat quarter felted wool (18″ × 22″)
OR
the equivalent, for 95–100 yards of fabric-yarn

NOTIONS

- Rotary cutter, ruler, and mat
- 1 spool of novelty thread to coordinate with the selected fabrics
- Small feathers to coordinate with fabrics
- Large-eye yarn needle
- Medium crochet hook (optional)
- Sewing needle
- Sewing thread to match fabrics

Preparation

Refer to Ready, Set, Let's Start Strippin' (pages 13–23).

Fabric-Yarns A-B-C-D-E: For each fabric, use a rotary cutter and a ruler to cut the fabrics crosswise into ¼″ strips. Keep the fabrics separated by color.

Make the fabric-yarn by joining 1 strip of each fabric-yarn in the order A to B to C to D to E. Join the strips with a continuous zigzag stitch, adding feathers to the strips by feeding them into the notch of the presser foot as you sew. Wind into 1 ball of fabric-yarn.

Fabrics for The Tippi

Add a bit of contrast to your hat by tipping The Tippi! Cast on and work the first row of the hat with a coordinating fabric-yarn before tying on the main color. A scrap of yarn about 4 yards long will do the trick.

Knitting

Work in a 1 × 1 rib (page 28) over an EVEN number of stitches. ODD rows are the right side of the work and EVEN rows are the wrong side.

CAST ON

Loosely cast on 48 stitches (S/M) [56 stitches (L/XL), 64 stitches (XXL)]. Instructions for the larger sizes appear in brackets.

ROW 1

Knit 1 stitch, and Purl 1 stitch. Repeat * to * across the remaining stitches, and end with a purl stitch.

CONTINUE KNITTING

Repeat Row 1 until the piece measures 6″ [7″, 8″]. End with an ODD row.

SHAPE HAT

The hat crown is created by decreasing stitches (page 29) every ODD row.

Decrease Row 1

Knit 1 stitch, and Purl 1 stitch for 6 stitches. Knit the next 2 stitches together. Repeat * to * 5 [6, 7] more times. (42 [49, 56] stitches on the needle.)

Decrease Row 2 and All EVEN Rows

Knit 1 stitch, and Purl 1 stitch. Repeat * to * across the remaining stitches.

Decrease Row 3

(Note: Repeat is worked over 7 stitches.)
Knit 1 stitch, and Purl 1 stitch for 5 stitches. Knit the next 2 stitches together. Repeat * to * 5 [6, 7] more times. (36 [42, 48] stitches on the needle.)

Decrease Rows 4, 6, 8, 10, and 12

Repeat Decrease Row 2.

Decrease Row 5

(Note: Repeat is worked over 6 stitches.)
Knit 1 stitch, and Purl 1 stitch for 4 stitches. Knit the next 2 stitches together. Repeat * to * 5 [6, 7] more times. (30 [35, 40] stitches on the needle.)

Decrease Row 7

(Note: Repeat is worked over 5 stitches.)
Knit 1 stitch, and Purl 1 stitch for 3 stitches. Knit the next 2 stitches together. Repeat * to * 5 [6, 7] more times. (24 [28, 32] stitches on the needle.)

Decrease Row 9

(Note: Repeat is worked over 4 stitches.)
Knit 1 stitch, and Purl 1 stitch. Knit the next 2 stitches together. Repeat * to * 5 [6, 7] more times. (18 [21, 24] stitches on the needle.)

Decrease Row 11

(Note: Repeat is worked over 3 stitches.)
Knit 1 stitch. Knit the next 2 stitches together. Repeat * to * 5 [6, 7] more times. (12 [14, 16] stitches on the needle.)

Decrease Row 13

Knit 2 stitches together. Repeat * to * 5 [6, 7] times. (6 [7, 8] stitches on the needle.)

Finishing

Refer to pages 33–35.

1. Cut the fabric-yarn from the ball, leaving approximately 12″ attached to the hat.
2. Thread the large-eye needle with the length of fabric-yarn attached to the hat. Use the yarn needle to slip off the remaining stitches from the knitting needle. Pull the fabric-yarn completely through the stitches.
3. With right sides together, sew the side seam closed using the needle and fabric-yarn. With each pass of the needle and fabric-yarn, catch 2 stitches—1 stitch from each side of the seam.
4. Use the needle or crochet hook to weave the loose tail ends of the fabric-yarn into the body of the work or along the finished edges.
5. If necessary, hide the ends of the fabric-yarn by using a sewing needle and thread to stitch them so they don't show.

Olivia Top

**Designed and knit by Olivia Booth
Sizes: Women's Extra Small
to Extra Large**

I named this beautiful tank top after my friend Olivia, who designed and knitted both pieces for the book. I especially like the simplicity of the form of the garment, which showcases the unique fabric-yarns used. The white top is cotton and uses the spatter dye technique described on page 11. The other is made of linen and polyester and is as light as a feather. The rib knit gives the Olivia Top lots of stretch. Worked on circular needles, knitting this garment is a snap.

What You'll Need

NEEDLES/GAUGE

Gauge (refer to page 32): 3 stitches per 1˝. Try size 10 ½ circular needles with a 16˝ or 24˝ cable, and adjust as needed.

The instructions are given for the extra-small size, which is a great tween or small adult size. The larger sizes are indicated in the knitting instructions in brackets.

FABRICS

Your yardage requirements may vary. Refer to Woven Fabric versus Knit Fabric (page 7) and Fabric-Yarn (page 14).

I would make this top again and again just too see how it looked knit up in many of the fabric-yarns previously used in this book. It would be clingy and slinky if made up in a knit like the one used to make the Braided Illusion Scarf (page 77). I would use just a single-strand yarn, producing a loosely knit top, with the glitter making this truly fun.

Fabric A: 2 yards 100% cotton quilting fabric, 44″–45″ wide [3 yards for the 2 largest sizes]

OR

Fabric B: 1½ yards linen/polyester blend, 60″ wide [2½ yards for the 2 largest sizes]

OR

the equivalent, for 300 yards of fabric-yarn [450 yards for the 2 largest sizes]

NOTIONS

- Rotary cutter, ruler, and mat
- Fabric glue
- Circular knitting needle, 16″ or 24″ cable, in size to match gauge
- Stitch markers
- Large stitch holder
- Large-eye yarn needle
- Medium crochet hook (optional)
- Sewing needle
- Sewing thread to match fabric-yarn
- Perle cotton thread to match fabric

Fabrics for the Olivia Top

Preparation

Refer to Ready, Set, Let's Start Strippin' (pages 13–23).

Fabric-Yarn A or B: Use a rotary cutter and a ruler to cut the fabric crosswise into ¼″ strips. Glue or tie the fabric strips together, and wind into 1 large and 1 slightly smaller ball of fabric-yarn.

Circular Knitting

The entire top is knit in the round on circular needles in a 1 x 1 rib (page 28) worked over an EVEN number of stitches. Keep the stitches in pattern, meaning Knit the knit stitches, and Purl the purl stitches. When knitting with circular needles, the side facing you as you knit is the right side of the work.

Bust measurement	32″–34″	36″–38″	40″–42″	44″–46″	48″–50″
Finished garment bust	26″	30″	34″	36″	38″

 The finished sizes look small but the rib knit has lots of stretch. The piece is designed to finish as a form-fitting top.

TIP from Mark

CAST ON

Very loosely cast on 78 [90, 102, 110, 114] stitches onto 1 circular needle.

ROW 1

Bring the 2 needles together as to knit, and place a stitch marker onto the right needle. Make sure the stitches are not twisted on the needle, then pick up the fabric-yarn and knit the first stitch off the left needle. This will connect the starting and ending stitches from the cast-on into a continuous circle. Purl the next stitch.

Continue working Knit 1, Purl 1 rib stitch until you reach the stitch marker (the start of the next row).

CONTINUE KNITTING

Continue circular knitting, using the 1 x 1 rib stitch, until the piece measures 12″ [12″, 14″, 14″, 16″].

THE BACK

Shape the Armholes

1. Starting at the stitch marker, bind off (page 33) the first 3 [4, 5, 6, 7] stitches. Keeping the 1 x 1 rib pattern, Knit across 35 [40, 45, 48, 49] stitches. Place the remaining 39 [45, 51, 55, 57] stitches on a stitch holder for later (front). Turn.

2. With the wrong side facing you, bind off (page 33) the first 3 [4, 5, 6, 7] stitches at the beginning of this row. Keeping the 1 x 1 rib pattern, work across the row. Turn.

3. With the right side facing you, continuing to work in the 1 x 1 rib, bind off 1 stitch at the beginning of the next row, and every row after this, until there are 25 [29, 33, 35, 35] stitches remaining on the needle.

4. Continue the 1 x 1 rib pattern across the 25 [29, 33, 35, 35] stitches, and knit until the piece measures 6″ [6½″, 6½″, 6¾″, 7″] from the bottom of the armhole. End with a wrong-side row.

Divide for the Back Straps

1. With the right side facing you, continue the 1 x 1 rib across 7 [7, 7, 9, 9] stitches (right strap). Bind off the next 11 [15, 19, 17, 17] stitches (neckline). Work the next 6 [6, 6, 8, 8] rib stitches (left strap). Turn.

2. With the wrong side facing you, work the 7 [7, 7, 9, 9] stitches of the left strap. Tie on (page 29) the second ball of fabric-yarn to the right strap at the neckline edge and work the 7 [7, 7, 9, 9] stitches. Turn.

3. Continue working the 2 sets of straps in the 1 x 1 rib, using separate balls of fabric-yarn for each. Knit until the straps measure 3″ [3″, 3″, 3½″, 3½″] from the bound-off stitches of the neckline.

4. Loosely bind off each strap.

THE FRONT

Shape the Armholes

1. Place the 39 [45, 51, 55, 57] stitches from the stitch holder onto the circular needle.

2. With the right side facing you, tie on fabric-yarn, and bind off the first 3 [4, 5, 6, 7] stitches at the beginning of this row. Keeping the 1 x 1 rib pattern, work across the row. Turn.

3. With the wrong side facing you, bind off the first 3 [4, 5, 6, 7] stitches at the beginning of this row. Keeping the 1 x 1 rib pattern, work across the row. Turn.

4. While continuing to work the 1 x 1 rib pattern, bind off 1 stitch at the beginning and end of every RIGHT SIDE row until 27 [31, 35, 37, 37] stitches remain.

5. Work the 27 [31, 35, 37, 37] stitches in the 1 x 1 rib until the piece measures 3½″ [4″, 4″, 4¼″, 4½″] from the bottom of the armhole. End with a wrong-side row.

Divide for the Front Straps

1. With the right side facing you, work 9 [9, 9, 11, 11] stitches (left strap). Bind off 9 [13, 17, 15, 15] stitches (neckline). Work the next 8 [8, 8, 10, 10] stitches (right strap). Turn.

2. With the wrong side facing you, work 9 [9, 9, 11, 11] stitches of the right strap. Attach the second ball of fabric-yarn to the left strap at the neckline edge and work the 9 [9, 9, 11, 11] stitches. Turn.

3. Continue working the 2 sets of straps with separate balls of fabric-yarn for each, binding off 1 stitch at the strap's neckline edge every RIGHT side row until 7 [7, 7, 9, 9] stitches remain per strap.

4. Continue to work the straps in 1 x 1 rib until they measure 5½″ [5½″, 5½″, 6″, 6″] from the bound-off stitches at the neckline.

5. Loosely bind off both of the straps.

Finishing

Refer to pages 33–35.

1. Use the large-eye needle and perle cotton thread to sew the front and back straps together, right sides facing.

2. Use the large-eye needle or crochet hook to weave the loose tail ends of the fabric-yarn into the body of the work or along the finished edges.

3. If necessary, hide the ends of the fabric-yarn by using a sewing needle and thread to stitch them so they don't show.

4. Block (page 34) the finished top.

A Selection of Three Embellishments

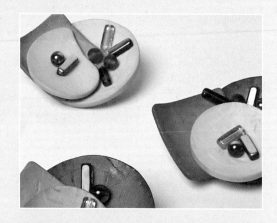

Button and Bead Pins

Cluster the buttons and add beads.

Finished size: varies depending on size of buttons

When I saw these buttons, I knew I had to use them for something special. Use the biggest buttons you can find— the largest here is 2¼"—and cluster them together to form interesting color patterns and shapes. I used three per grouping because I wanted to show off the offbeat shapes and luscious colors of the buttons, and I chose glass beads to enhance the embellishment.

What You'll Need

- An assortment of large buttons, 3–5 per cluster
- Glass beads
- Glue that bonds glass and plastic, such as Weldbond Universal Adhesive
- Pin backs

Make the Pin

1. Arrange 3 to 5 buttons in a cluster.
2. Glue the buttons in your chosen order. Allow the glue to dry.
3. Glue the glass beads onto the button cluster. Allow the glue to dry.

 TIP from Mark *After you decide on an arrangement in a cluster, take a close-up digital snapshot so you can glue the buttons back in sequence.*

4. On the reverse side, glue a pin back to the button cluster. Allow the glue to dry.

 TIP from Mark *If the undersides of your buttons are not flat, use a pair of needle-nose pliers to gently bend the pin back so it conforms to the curve.*

Back of pin

Felt and Fabric Floral Pins

Finished size: 3″ × 3″

The technique for creating these folk-art-looking fused and felted pins allows you to make several pins at a time. Minimal sewing skills are required, but sewing can be eliminated entirely by using decorative glue instead.

This is a great project to make from scraps, so don't forget to save all those small, usable pieces.

What You'll Need

FABRIC

- Scraps of cotton fabrics large enough for template pieces (page 90)
- Scraps of natural-fiber felt or felted wool

NOTIONS

- 1 sheet template plastic or cardboard
- ¼ yard paper-backed fusible web
- Iron
- Coordinating thread to be used decoratively
- Straight-edge scissors
- Pinking shears (optional)
- Craft glue
- Glitter glue or puff paint (optional)
- Pin backs or clip attachments

Preparation

Following the manufacturer's instructions, iron the fusible web to the wrong side of the cotton fabric. Let it cool, and peel off the paper backing. Place the fused cotton piece on top of the felt, and fuse the layers. Allow the fused pieces to cool. Repeat as many times as needed to prepare the materials for either single or multiple pins.

Fuse together the felt and cotton.

Make the Pin

1. Trace the flower and leaf patterns (page 90) onto the template plastic or cardboard. Cut them out.

2. Center the templates on the wrong (felt) side of the fused cotton and felt. Trace the pattern. Repeat as necessary.

3. Cut out the pieces. Pieces with pinked edges are cut so the bottom of the pinked edge is touching the traced line.

4. With a sewing machine, add decorative stitching to individual pieces before assembly. Decorative stitching can be replaced with glitter glue or puff paint. Follow the manufacturer's instructions, and allow the pieces to dry thoroughly before proceeding.

5. Put a spot of glue in the center of each piece, and layer the pieces as shown. Allow the glue to dry.

6. Glue the pin back or clip to the back of the layered flower. Allow the glue to dry.

Cut out the fused fabric.

Stitch with decorative stitching or decorate with paint.

Layer and glue.

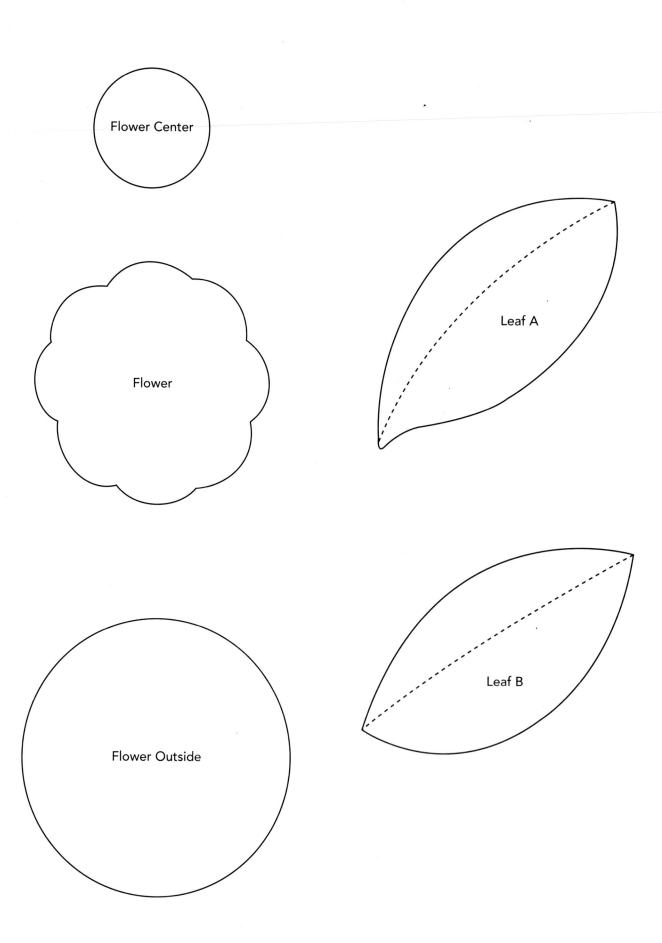

Flower Center

Flower

Leaf A

Flower Outside

Leaf B

Strip & Knit with Style

Seed Bead Starfish

Finished sizes: 3½″ × 3½″ and 4″ × 4″

These brightly colored starfish, which seem to be jumping for joy, can be pinned to a wide a variety of projects. Used on pillows they add a cluster of sparkle here and there. Use one as a clasp to keep your scarf closed, or as an adornment for a lapel or hat brim. Fill a glass bowl with starfish as a centerpiece, or use them to decorate gift packages. The uses for these fun embellishments are endless.

These are addictive to make, and when it comes time to glue on the beads, the process reminds me of decorating cookies in colorful sugar crystals.

What You'll Need

FABRIC

- Cotton fabric, 2 pieces 5″ × 5″ for small starfish, or 2 pieces 6″ × 6″ for large starfish

 TIP from Mark *Scraps work well here, and the top of the starfish can be a different color from the bottom.*

NOTIONS

- 1 sheet template plastic or cardboard
- ¼ yard fusible knit interfacing
- Thread to match fabrics
- Small scissors
- Sewing needles
- Crochet hook or other long, blunt object to aid in turning starfish inside out
- Polyester fiberfill
- Craft glue
- Paintbrush
- Assorted seed beads or similar small beads
- Pin backs or clip attachments

Make the Starfish

1. Trace the starfish patterns (page 93) onto template plastic or cardboard. Cut them out.
2. Cut 2 pieces of fusible knit interfacing the same size as your cut fabric pieces.
3. Following the manufacturer's instructions, fuse the knit interfacing to the wrong side of the cut fabric pieces.

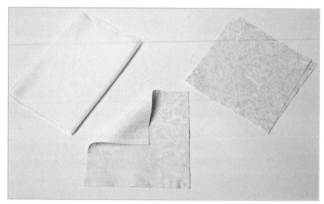

Fuse the interfacing to the fabric.

4. Center the template on the wrong side of 1 piece of fused fabric. Trace the pattern onto the interfacing side.

Pin together the fused fabric.

5. Place the right sides together, and pin the fused pieces around the outside of the traced design and on the inside of the starfish arms.

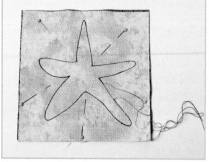

Sew together the pieces.

6. Use a very small stitch and sew on top of the traced line. Start and stop on the inside of an arm, leaving a ½″ to ¾″ opening for turning. Remove the pins.

7. Trim away the excess fabric, leaving a scant ⅛″ seam allowance. Clip the seam allowances in the V corners of the arms.
8. Start with the arm of the starfish that is opposite the opening, and use a crochet hook or turning tool to push the tip of the arm into the body of the starfish. Stop when it is half turned. Repeat for the other 4 arms.

Start turning the starfish right side out.

9. Push the arm opposite the opening completely through the opening. Use the turning tool to push the other 4 arms through.
10. Use the turning tool pushed through the opening from the inside. Gently push the arms out until they are completely turned.

Finish turning the starfish right side out.

11. Use small bits of fiberfill to stuff the tips of the arms, then the main part of the arms, and finally the body of the starfish.

Stuff the starfish.

12. With matching thread and a sewing needle, slip-stitch the opening closed.

13. Put the beads into a small dish. Use the paint-brush to apply a coating of craft glue to one side of the starfish body. Dip the glued side in the beads. Let the glue dry. Repeat the process, if necessary, to fill in any gaps or holes in the glued bead surface.

Glue beads to the starfish.

14. Glue the pin back or clip to the underside of the starfish body.

Large Starfish

Small Starfish

Resources

CUTTING TOOLS

Alto's EZ Mat, Inc.
Alto's QuiltCut2 Fabric Cutting System
703 N. Wenas Street
Ellensburg, WA 98926
(800) 225-2497 / (509) 962-9212
www.quiltcut.com

Townsend Industries
Townsend Fabric Cutter
P.O. Box 97
Altoona, IA 50009
(877) 868-3544 / (515) 967-4261
www.townsendfabriccutter.com

FABRIC AND NOTIONS

Blank Textiles
Cotton fabric
65 W. 36th Street
New York, NY 10018
(888) 442-5265 / (212) 563-6225
www.blanktextiles.com
(Wholesale only; products available in quilt and fabric shops)

Dill Buttons of America, Inc.
Buttons
50 Choate Circle
Montoursville, PA 17754
(888) 460-7555 / (560) 368-0660
www.dill-buttons.com
(Wholesale only; products available in quilt and fabric shops)

Frank T. Ross & Sons, Inc.
Weldbond glue
6550 Lawrence Avenue East
Toronto, ON M1C 4A7
Canada
(414) 282-1107 / (414) 282-8150
www.weldbond.com

Gütermann
Beads, thread
www.gutermann.com
(Wholesale only; products available in quilt and fabric shops)

JoAnn Stores
Fabrics (cotton, polar fleece, waffle-knit fleece, and faux fur), precut fabric strips, notions, knitting needles
www.JoAnn.com

Lantern Moon
Silk Gelato precut fabric strips, knitting needles, baskets
7911 N.E. 33rd Drive, Suite 140
Portland, OR 97211
(800) 530-4170 / (503) 460-0003
www.lanternmoon.com
(Wholesale only; visit the website for retail locations)

Logantex, Inc.
Ombré and novelty sheer fabrics
70 W. 36th Street
New York, NY 10018
(212) 221-3900
www.logantex.com
(Wholesale only)

Mary Flanagan Woolens
Hand-dyed felted woolen fabrics
(920) 589-2221
www.mfwoolens.com

Michael Miller Fabrics
Fairy Frost and Mirror Ball Dot cotton fabric
118 W. 23rd Street
New York, NY 10011
(212) 704-0774
www.michaelmillerfabrics.com
(Wholesale only; visit the website for retail locations)

Michael's
Fabric (cotton, nylon mesh lace, and cotton flannel), precut fabric strips, notions, knitting needles
www.michaels.com

N.Y. Elegant Fabrics
Fabric
222 W. 40th Street
New York, NY 10018
(212) 302-4984 / (212) 302-4996
(Wholesale and retail)

Princess Mirah Design / Bali Fabrics, Inc.
Batik cotton, rayon, and flannel fabric; precut fabric strips
21787 Eighth Street East, Suite #1
Sonoma, CA 95476
(800) 783-4612
www.balifab.com
(Wholesale only; visit the website for retail locations)

Rosen & Chadick
Fashion fabrics, luxury fibers
561 Seventh Avenue (corner of 40th Street)
2nd and 3rd Floors
New York, NY 10018
(800) 225-3838 / (212) 869-0142
www.rosenandchadickfabrics.com

Sulky of America
Thread, stabilizers
980 Cobb Place Blvd., Suite 130
Kennesaw, GA 30144
(800) 874-4115
www.sulky.com
(Wholesale only; visit the website for retail locations)

Woodstock Quilt Supply
Complete collection of Fairy Frost fabric
79 Tinker Street
Woodstock, NY 12498
(845) 679-0733
www.quiltstock.com
(Online retail store)

For a list of other fine books from C&T Publishing, ask for a free catalog:
C&T Publishing, Inc.
P.O. Box 1456
Lafayette, CA 94549
(800) 284-1114
Email: ctinfo@ctpub.com
Website: www.ctpub.com
C&T Publishing's professional photography services are now available to the public.
Visit us at www.ctmediaservices.com.

For quilting supplies:
Cotton Patch
1025 Brown Ave.
Lafayette, CA 94549
(800) 835-4418 or
(925) 283-7883
Email: CottonPa@aol.com
Website: www.quiltusa.com

Note: Fabrics used in the items shown may not be currently available, as fabric manufacturers keep most fabrics in print for only a short time.

About the Author

A native New Yorker, Mark spent two years studying at the Culinary Institute of America in Hyde Park, New York, after he graduated from high school. He has been in both the front and back of the house as chef, sous-chef, and maître d', and in 1983 was awarded an honorable mention for his bread sculpture at the 114th Annual Salon of Culinary Arts.

Half a decade later, Mark chose to pursue his second career in menswear and attended the Fashion Institute of Technology (FIT).

Mark's innate color sense and use of patterns and textures were rewarded during his years at FIT with a number of scholarships and the Designer's Critic Award at graduation. In 1989, Mark had the opportunity to design neckwear for Hermès, and was given a two-week internship at the design studio in Paris after winning the Comité Colbert L'Art de Vivre award for menswear and redesigning the uniforms for the NYC Staten Island Ferry crew.

After graduating from FIT, he took a position as an assistant designer for a thriving New York–based sweater company and headed the private-label division for five years. A textile project for a friend led to a design position at a major fabric converter, where he was responsible for merchandising customer and licensee accounts as well as designing for the open line.

Next it was time for Mark to start his own business ventures, and in 2002 he was awarded Cotton Inc.'s 21st Annual Cotton Incorporated Textile Designer's Award for outstanding contributions to innovative design and styling in the Prints – Home category.

Mark is the creator of the Mirror Ball Dot and Rock Candy fabric lines. His Fairy Frost fabric line has sold over 2 million yards to date. He is currently licensing his designs on cotton to two New York–based textile companies for quilting, crafting, and manufacturing. Recent projects include the self-publication of his first novel, *Shag* (www.shagthemammoth.com); his collaboration with a documentary filmmaker/producer and animation studio as artistic director on an original concept for a television series; and plans for his own line of neckwear.

Great Titles from C&T PUBLISHING

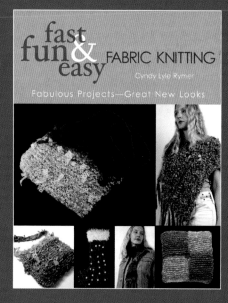

fast fun & easy FABRIC KNITTING
Cyndy Lyle Rymer
Fabulous Projects—Great New Looks

Indygo Junction's Needle Felting
22 Stylish Projects for Home & Fashion
Amy Barickman

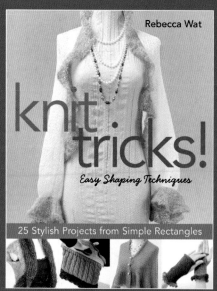

Rebecca Wat

knit tricks!
Easy Shaping Techniques
25 Stylish Projects from Simple Rectangles

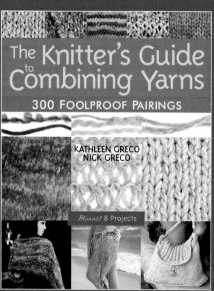

The Knitter's Guide to Combining Yarns
300 FOOLPROOF PAIRINGS
KATHLEEN GRECO
NICK GRECO
Bonus! 8 Projects

Available at your local retailer or
www.ctpub.com or 800.284.1114